AMBER NINE

Back in the liquidating business, Boysie Oakes finds himself on the sunny shores of Lake Maggiore, where he is to ensure that a Member of Parliament breathes his last, but things go horribly wrong and Boysie is pulled into the biggest espionage foul-up of the century. Precipitated into a flash finishing school run by Doctor Klara Thirel, fair, thirty and sadistic, Boysie finds girlies galore, among them a certain Petronella Whitching...

AMBER NINE

AMBER NINE

by

John Gardner

Magna Large Print Books
Long Preston, North Yorkshire,
BD23 4ND, England.

British Library Cataloguing in Publication Data.

Gardner, John
    Amber nine.

    A catalogue record of this book is
    available from the British Library

    ISBN   0-7505-2352-2

First published in Great Britain in 1966 by
Frederick Muller Ltd.

Copyright © 1966 Boysie Oakes Ltd.

The moral right of the author has been asserted

Published in Large Print 2005 by arrangement with
John Gardner, care of Coombs Moylett Literary Agency

Magna Large Print is an imprint of Library Magna Books Ltd.

Printed and bound in Great Britain by
T.J. (International) Ltd., Cornwall, PL28 8RW

For Elizabeth

I should like to acknowledge the invaluable technical data given me by Captain E. Mercer, D.F.C., and John W. Young, Jnr.

Things are seldom what they seem,
Skim milk masquerades as cream.

H.M.S. PINAFORE: Sir W. S. Gilbert

Contents

PROLOGUE

LOCATION CLASSIFIED

The knife was exactly 20.32 centimetres long. At its widest point – near the bone hilt – it measured 1.27 centimetres, and the blade had been blackened over a smoky candle so there was no danger of its glint being picked up in the darkness. The soldier never knew what happened. Just a second of unimaginable pain slamming through the back. For all he knew it could have been a heart attack. There was not even time to cry out.

The man they called Phentos regretted having to kill the soldier, but he had planned well – picking the night that this particular man was on duty. The soldier, known to have many enemies here, was already down for posting away from the maximum security area. In the morning, when they found him, his death would be put down to an internal incident.

Phentos dragged the body behind the

angled wall of the concrete bunker. The wall sheltered them, the living and the dead. It was a relief to hide for a moment. The night was charity cold – an east wind slicing up from the sea, singing round the gantries a mile and a half away across the flat stretch of land. That was the eternal sound of this wilderness which reached up into the stratosphere: the sound Phentos would carry to his grave – the shriek of wind round the gantries, a siren song. Phentos hugged the wall. Far away – among the cluster of huts that was the experiment section – a rocket motor started up. Probably an all-night test. The beast would roar until the early hours, spitting its great sheet of flame against the metal shield until it turned white hot.

Phentos looked at his watch. Eleven fifty-five. Time to move into the bunker. Slowly he edged round the corner of the wall. A flurry of light snow struck his face, stinging like a handful of nettles. Down the steps and up to the steel door which, until a few moments before, had been guarded by the soldier. He moved carefully and with a precision born from hours of patient rehearsal with a stop watch. He had to be through the door at exactly eleven fifty-eight. The luminous hand on his wristwatch dial jerked up to the minute. Phentos pressed down on the handle and put his shoulder against the door. The big slab of metal did not move. Two seconds. Then, noiselessly it swung under his weight. The main Tracking Room door – at the far end of the bunker – had been opened to allow the tracking staff to change watch. All the doors in the bunker were operated by the same switch. Phentos had two minutes. The electronic locks were off for two minutes during the staff change.

Down the passage and through the door on the right. Into the long cell which was the Programme Store. He crossed to the line of metal racks which covered the far wall. Twenty seconds. A gloved index finger slid along the numbered tags above the racks. It stopped at the required serial. Thirty seconds. He checked the number. Thirty-five seconds. The hand slipped into the rack and removed the metal spool. Forty seconds. Already the duplicate was out from the inside of his jacket. Phentos switched the spools. Fifty seconds.

Now, over to the far end of the room. The same procedure with the second serial number they had given him. Eighty seconds. A last check to make sure the two programming spools were snug in the webbing container stitched into his jacket. Eighty-five seconds. Over to the door. Out. Door closed. Along the passage. Out. Close. Lean against the wall. Breathe deeply. Through the nose. Even in the cold he was sweating hard. Out. Out – with time to spare. One hundred and fifteen seconds. One hundred and twenty seconds. The whirr as the electronic locks came into play. Shut safe. No alarm bells. In the Tracking Room the new shift settled down in front of their radar screens and the computers – locked in for the night.

At the main gate the guard nodded, took his ID pass with the punch marks and concealed wire pattern, and fed it into the checking machine. The green light came on. OK. The guard knew him well enough but there was a rigid adherence to the routine security system – it was foolproof.

'Goodnight, Captain Phentos,' said the guard.

Phentos nodded. His usual surly way. The guard watched the stubby little figure waddling off up the road to the officers' quarters and thought evil thoughts. The wind screamed through the rigging of the gantries. The rocket motor continued to roar, and two vital spools of tape were on their way out of the country.

CHAPTER ONE

RED TARGET: LONDON

Boysie Oakes banged down on the clutch, flipped the gear stick into second, released the clutch and applied firm pressure on the brake pedal. The long sexy white nose of the 4-2 E-type slid dangerously close to the rear fender of a grey Ford van – the property of an exorbitantly expensive Bond Street couturier. Boysie voiced an unlikely deviationist act against the Minister of Transport. To the right, a taxi driver leered from his cab: the look spelled out b-l-o-o-d-y c-a-p-i-t-a-l-i-s-t. To the left, a young woman, at the wheel of a blue NSU Prinz Sports, examined her eye shadow and found it wanting. Boysie glanced into his driving mirror. It was filled with a dirty radiator across which the word BEDFORD gleamed in chrome.

Mostyn was right. Only a pig-headed fool would drive a Jaguar from Chesham Place to Whitehall and back again, morning and evening, in this sort of traffic. The tin phalanx of vehicles moved forward for two yards and stopped again.

'Rot the Minister! He'll have to go!' said Boysie.

'Hey, mate, you ought to trade that in for a motor scooter,' shouted the taxi driver. Boysie pretended not to hear. It had been like this for six months. Hemmed in by traffic night and morning – feeling like a stuffed twit with the rolled umbrella and curly brimmed bowler on the passenger seat – then hemmed in by Mostyn all day. Six months. It had been a hard winter. In retrospect, Boysie could not make up his mind which was the lesser evil – facing the terrors, and personal deceit, of operational life, or the endless niggle of being Personal Assistant to the Second-in-Command.

Since the American escapade, Mostyn had held Boysie to him as though by grappling irons.

'Chief says it'll do you good to have a spell actually working here in Department HQ, old Boysie,' he said when Boysie reported back from leave.

Disenchanted, Boysie had muttered, 'What as? Your Chief Whip?'

Mostyn managed a sly smile. 'Mental

flagellation's more in my line. You ought to know that by now, laddie.' The smile was tailored in Bri-Nylon. A set of immaculate fingernails rested on Boysie's charcoal-grey flannel sleeve.

'You're coming to me. As my PA,' said Mostyn. 'Won't that be super?'

So the winter started, with Boysie doing his daily drive to the Whitehall building. It was a month before he was able to capture a regular parking space. Even that was a good five-minutes' walk from the solid swing doors which led into the dull, uninviting foyer – tastefully decorated in Ministry of Works green and lavatory-type tiles – which served as a front to the Headquarters of the British Department of Special Security.

The morning routine rarely varied. Across the foyer, with a nod to the commissionaire. Into the lift permanently marked OUT OF ORDER. Key into the door at the back of the lift, and through on to the blue Wilton of Reception – chrome and glass, strip-lighting and a bold Paul Klee abstract. Nod to the receptionist. Into the lift and up – past GIR on the first, and Operations on the second – to the third floor: the Executive Area.

For Boysie, being Mostyn's PA was like

living in an eternal death cell. Never knowing a moment's peace of mind. Constantly
anxious and listening for the step outside the
door. Everyone affirmed that Mostyn was a
splendid professional, but he was also a man
motivated by the devil of sadism. For many
years now, Boysie had been Mostyn's pet
obsession – mainly because Boysie Oakes
was one of the few men who had
unknowingly succeeded in really worrying
Mostyn. It was understandable. At the time
of his recruitment, Boysie was the hottest
thing the 2 I/C had ever handled. When the
Department had desperately needed
someone to thin out the weeds of security
risks, Mostyn, in his omnipotence, had
picked Boysie, trained him, coated him with
the plastic veneer of near-sophistication and
sent him into the field as a bludgeon, a
private headsman, who stalked death
through the corridors of subversion. Boysie's
very existence within the Department had
been a liability. In those early days, when
Boysie was working as Chief Liquidating
Agent, Mostyn knew full well that it would
be his own head that would roll gently from
the political guillotine if the true nature of
Boysie's occupation ever became public
knowledge. The Chief would never admit

responsibility. Owning a lethal weapon (like Boysie) with Government permission was one thing, Mostyn used to tell himself. Owning him without official sanction was quite another matter. As the years went by Mostyn had become more concerned. At times he even found it hard to believe that the brash and artless Boysie could dispense death with such ease. In the end it was a relief to find that circumstances dictated taking 'L' (Boysie's Security Designation) off the liquidating assignments.

If Mostyn had only known it, no one was happier at this turn of events than Boysie. To be removed from the shadowy status of murderer without portfolio had been his pipe dream since the whole nightmare began. Yet the change of work brought no relief to his personal fear, and deep-seated hatred of Mostyn – who still seemed to regard himself as Boysie's puppeteer-god. As for Mostyn, Boysie still remained the major itch which played hide-and-seek with his conscience, jerking him from sleep and causing nervous disorders, the like of which Mostyn had never known. Boysie in the field – even on the most simple courier job – could inflict grave doubts and unaccountable headaches.

By keeping Boysie close, and within eye and earshot, Mostyn hoped to lay the ghost of his deep feelings of responsibility towards the man. In fact the appointment as PA to the 2 I/C only made matters worse. In close contact with one another the odd-love-hate relationship began to rise towards its fully combustible potential. Within a week the mere fact of Boysie's presence began to exasperate Mostyn. Then he started to probe into 'L's' executive inefficiency. Boysie reacted by turning awkward – becoming bovine in attitude and stabbing at Mostyn by perpetrating small acts of violence: like rearranging the papers and ornaments on the 2 I/C's normally impeccable desk. Whereupon Mostyn put the boot in. He harried Boysie, chipped away at his nerve-ends using every trick he knew. And Mostyn's knowledge of tricks was considerable. He was reputed to be one of the best interrogators in the business.

Each night on his way home, frustrated by jammed traffic, Boysie would sit in the Jaguar and go over the events of the day. To unwind, he would use his old dodge – methodically cursing Mostyn with a string of obscene and pertinent invective. This seldom failed to clear his mind and brush away a little of the humiliation and one-downmanship which was his usual condition after a few hours spent with Colonel James George Mostyn. With the mind in a more lucid frame he could then go on to invent sharp rejoinders to comments which, during the hours of business, had been one-sided and cutting – in Mostyn's favour. But tonight, flanked by the taxi driver and the lady with the mascara problem, Boysie suddenly realised that this day had been different. Yesterday, all hell was let loose. But today, life had been almost idyllic.

Perhaps, thought Boysie, it was the spring. Certainly it was a warmer day. The girl from Records looked more full-busted. The sap was rising. In the lunch hour he noticed that buds were in evidence in St James's Park. Perhaps Mostyn was in love. Mostyn's complex, and rather helixical, associations with the opposite sex could rarely be docketed as 'love affairs'. Really they were more in the nature of 'love affrays'. Yet, to Boysie's certain knowledge, he had of late been seeing a lot of Janet Scampini the model – and there was a lot of Janet Scampini to be seen.

This line of reasoning took Boysie's thoughts automatically to Elizabeth. Boysie smiled. Elizabeth had been the one worth-while thing during the great hard winter battle with Mostyn. But then Elizabeth was special – which was saying something, as Boysie's taste in women lay in the gourmet class. His particular mode of life lifted him into a very specialised sphere. Blondes, brunettes, red-heads, tall, sinuous, lithe, gorgeous, well-connected, well-furbished, custom-built, smart, intelligent and exclusively desirable. Boysie had them all. They came, and went, violently, quietly, singing, laughing and crying. But, over the last two years, Boysie had always returned to Elizabeth. Whatever else was going on (or coming off) Elizabeth was somewhere in the background – barely twenty-five, short, snub-nosed, tied to her job as a typist at the Board of Trade, and with no pretensions to sophistication. Elizabeth was alive, and with her Boysie never had to pretend, or hide his most excruciating fears. On summer week-ends their haunts were in the Cotswolds among the dry stone walls and sweeping fields of barley. When they were together in London they did not meet in Boysie's favourite polished bars or glittering synthetic hotel lounges. Instead, they discovered the lost places and silent things. Boysie never

thought of their relationship as one of love –
more as a series of peaceful interludes of
discovery, spiced with great moments which
were purely physical. As for Elizabeth, she
adored Boysie and came like an arrow when
called. This time she had been called just
before Christmas.

A vast hooting or horns woke Boysie from
his daydream. The traffic was moving again
and BEDFORD appeared to be trying to work
its way up the twin exhaust pipes. The Jaguar
purred forwards, thrusting towards
Chesham Place and Elizabeth.

Boysie was whistling the open phrase from
the Bartok Third, for Piano and Orchestra,
as he pushed home his Yale key. *Toki's Theme*
from *Brubeck's Impressions of Japan* slid from
the record player, and Boysie's interpret-
ation caused Bartok to lose on points.
Elizabeth was in the kitchen wrestling with
Clement Freud.

'How's me old Mrs Beeton then?' gushed
Boysie.

'"Do not stir the rice until it is cooked and
the surface pitted with evenly spaced inden-
tations!"' Elizabeth read carefully from the
Sunday colour supplement propped by the
gas stove. 'It doesn't matter if I stir or not. It
goes soggy on me just the same.'

'Not chopsticks night again is it?' Boysie buried his lips in her short black hair and bit tenderly into the back of her neck. Elizabeth still concentrated.

'Paella. "With fish or any crustacean you care to add" it says here. Which means that de luxe tin of crabmeat you've been hoarding.'

'But that's *Bon Vivant Crab Newburg*. You'll ruin it. It was for rainy days.'

'It poured this morning. Teemed.' She turned and put her arms round his neck. 'Didn't it teem this morning, darling?'

'My bloody tin of *Crab Newburg*. I was saving it,' Boysie grinned and kissed. Big reaction. Then Elizabeth drew away.

'You can't,' she said. 'Anyway, I want to talk to you. It's rather important.'

'Oh?' Boysie allowed himself to be led out of the kitchen and guided to the *chaise-longue* – 'one of the most suggestive pieces of furniture ever invented' someone had once written.

'Actually, darling, it's a bit serious.' She was standing in front of him, legs apart. Eyes open to maximum, the little snub nose shining above almost negroid lips.

'Shoot.' Boysie put on his understanding smile.

29

'It's a bit difficult...'

'Who is the dog? I'll horse-whip him.'

'No, please, Boysie. I think I'm pregnant.'

'You're what!' A kind of ruptured roar. 'What? Again you think you're pregnant? That's three times in three months. Every month we have the same story, and every month it's the same answer – two days later, "Darling, I was wrong I'm not pregnant after all."'

'Well.' A pout.

'Yes. Well. Don't be half-baked, Liz. You know that nobody in the Department has ever got a girl in the club. It's unthinkable. Just doesn't happen. Have you ever known it happen? Even with the really flash boys it doesn't happen. Unwritten law. You've never heard of Dick or James or Harry putting a girl up the loop. Now get the paella.' He stood up, turned her round by the shoulders, gently smacked her bottom, then sat down again to brood on the phenomenon of Mostyn's good temper. Mostyn's pleasantness during the day made him more uneasy than Mostyn at full verbal slash. It could be neither spring nor love, he decided. Knowing Mostyn it just had to be something more sinister.

The telephone rang as they sat down to

dinner. The bell seemed to have acquired an unusually harsh note. Boysie knew who was at the other end before he heard the smarmed-down accent, leaning slightly back on itself, through the earpiece.

'L?' asked Mostyn.

'Yes.' Gingerly.

'You left the office a bit smartish tonight, old boy.'

Oh well, thought Boysie, it could not last for ever. This was the Mostyn he knew.

'You said you were going to be in conference with the Chief. You said you'd be late,' he tried.

'So I did, but that doesn't mean you've got to start watching the clock does it? Actually I'd hoped this would wait until the morning. It's "pressure", old lad.'

Boysie seemed to have lost the power of speech. It was a along time since he had heard the word 'pressure'. In the old days it was his code alert that a 'kill' was imminent.

'It's what?'

'Pressure. The real McCoy...'

'But you said. You promised. You said I wouldn't have to do one of those again. Not ever, you said.'

'Now don't start shedding the old wool. I promised nothing. I said that I hoped you

31

would not be required in this capacity – after *Coronet* when your cover was broken. I don't want you to do it. But there's no other way. Sorry to take you from any other little plans, but it's a Red Target.' Red was the special-urgency prefix.

'But what about my replacement. Only the other day you were telling me how happy you were with him. Trying to needle me. I haven't done one of these in two years. I'm out of practice. I'm damned if I'm going to do one now.'

'You don't want to break your contract with us do you, old son? Durance vile that would mean. Incarceration. Nasty damp cells. Warders queening it over you. If you'd kept to the Department training programme instead of consorting all the time you'd feel a lot better about it – and so would I.'

There was a silence along the lonely telephone cable. Boysie's mind was clocking up 120 m.p.h. on a small-radius circuit. Mostyn spoke again.

'Matter of fact your replacement's got a touch of the 'flu. Got his feet wet last week in Scotland. You must have read about it. That poor little Naval Attaché on leave from the Belgrade Embassy. On a fishing holiday. He got wet as well. Lots of space in the nationals and about ten inches in the *Glasgow Evening News.*' Mostyn was cooing now. Then the tone changed. 'Look, lad, if you're not over at Briefing within half-an-hour I'm going to have you. To the hilt I'm going to have you. We'll give you the Guy Fawkes treatment – and you know what happened to Guy Fawkes.' Boysie did know what had happened to Guy Fawkes, in all its revolting detail. Mostyn was quite capable of doing the same to him – with trimmings.

'You with me "L"? Be a good fellow and move. You have to be on a plane first thing in the morning.' The line died with a sharp click dissolving into the dialling tone.

'Oh Christ,' blasphemed Boysie.

Elizabeth was sitting looking at him, her eyes asking a dozen questions.

'It's all happening,' said Boysie. 'With my luck you could be pregnant after all.'

'You've got to go away again.' A statement. Elizabeth's voice flat and unemotional.

Boysie nodded. His mind had turned into a set of hands – scrawny and reaching out, groping at the straws of ideas, fumbling, trying to plait them into a cohesive whole.

'I'd better go back to Hammersmith then,' said Elizabeth staring at her untouched paella congealing into a solid colourful lump on the plate.

'Yes.' Far away, not with her. Then 'Yes, I suppose so. Not tonight though. I've got to go out, but I'll be back. I leave tomorrow.'

'Can't you tell me?' It was just something to say. She knew him well enough to detect the mounting tide of anxiety. Elizabeth never pried as a rule. Vaguely she knew that Boysie's work was connected with stealth, but it was better to remain ignorant of the details. Boysie shook his head.

'Mostyn!' He spoke like an amateur warlock with pins held ready to stab a plasticine effigy.

'Better telephone Sandy and tell her I'll be coming back to the hovel tomorrow,' said Elizabeth. She forced herself to make a small explosive laugh sound. 'That'll shake her. She'll be up half the night washing my things she's been wearing.'

'Not for a minute. I'll have to use the phone.' He stretched out his hand, but the instrument began to ring before he reached the receiver.

'Hallo.'

'You not left yet, Boysie? Come on, lad, I'm on my way.' Mostyn's voice sword-blading it in his ear. Then the clock and dialling tone. Boysie looked at his watch.

'Oh gawd!' It was almost a real prayer. Why didn't he have the guts to get down to Special Briefing now, face Mostyn and tell him the truth? The times he had tried to tell him and failed. He should have known it would happen again one day – all the nerves and uncertainty and the fact of death swilling around him. Time was getting short. They would not give him the chance to mull over the morality of it. Action. He had to take some action.

'Back in the old routine,' he muttered. Inexplicably a Technicolor movie flashed on to the narrow screen of his mind. A double-act – straw boaters, white flannels, striped blazers and whirling canes against a painted backdrop with an audience roaring its head off. In the front row of the stalls sat Mostyn laughing like a lunatic. The double-act was going through a soft shoe shuffle. The fantasy camera inside his head closed on the nimble feet and tracked upwards to the faces. The double-act was himself and Griffin. He had to get Griffin. Lord help us he may have gone out of business. Changed his address even. The *Coronet* affair. Two years ago. He had seen Griffin once since then. A sunny day in Winchcombe – on one of their Cotswolds expeditions. They had

35

been looking at the church. One of the gargoyles reminded him of someone. Walking down the path between the bodies laid to rest under Betjemanesque tombstones – Elizabeth was laughing at some quip (about the gargoyle?) – he had raised his head and there was Griffin padding towards them. They looked at each other, and for a suspended moment Boysie thought the ex-undertaker was going to speak. But Griffin was a professional, a real old trouper in his macabre trade. He had not even nodded. The insecurity followed him for a fortnight – chipping away in his subconscious until he was almost convinced that Griffin had been employed by someone – Mostyn maybe – to put an end to things. To give him the grave treatment.

Boysie still had the telephone receiver in his hand. The old routine after a 'pressure' call. Phone Griffin, meet him, set up the deal, put the finger on the customer and leave the horror to Griffin. Then the pay-off. This was the sub-contracted liquidating double-act which Boysie had worked on the Department during that incredible time when his natural aversion to death, in any form, prevented him from actually carrying out the ultimate moments of the kill assignments. And it was still Boysie's secret. Boysie's and Griffin's.

His stomach felt like a family-pack casata as he dialled the number – coming back to him like an old, trusted, friend. Someone lifted the receiver at the other end and a voice he did not recognise, young and feminine, recited the number.

'Mr Griffin,' said Boysie. 'Can I speak to Mr Griffin?'

'E's owt oim afraid. Ooo is thet callin'?'

Boysie ignored the question. 'When do you expect him back? It's rather urgent.'

'Any tame neow reely.'

What a repulsive accent, he thought. Large dollops of Mostyn's highly superior attitude to his fellow men had been injected into Boysie. For most of the time he kept them at bay, but, at moments like this, they came gurgling to the surface, all smarmy and snide.

'Could you give him a message?'

'Yeas.'

Normally Boysie would not have risked it, but there was no other way.

'Would you tell him Mr Oakes called – O-A-K-E-S. He'll remember me. Mr Oakes. Tell him I must see him urgently. It's business. If he would call me as soon as he gets in. He knows the number. I have to go out but there will be somebody here. OK?'

'All rate. Ey'll tell 'im.'

'Thank you.'

'Is that all?'

'Yes. Thank you very much. Thank you.'

'Bay-bay.'

'Bay-bay,' mimicked Boysie when the line cleared. 'Sounds as if old Griffin's been whoring up the 'dilly. Sorry, Liz love. It's absolute hell. Mostyn's a...'

'I know, Boysie. I know what Mostyn is. You've told me.'

'Yes.' Boysie got up.

'Can I warm your paella for you?'

Boysie could not have kept down an invalid's pre-digested Bath bun, let alone the spicy paella.

'I'm not terribly hungry, darling. Anyway, got to go. Queen-and-Country as my lovable boss would say.'

He wandered into the hall and shrugged his shoulders into the heavy suede car coat with the fur collar.

'You look beautiful, darling,' said Elizabeth making all light-hearted and loving.

But Boysie was wrapped in a shroud of personal misery.

'Have you got to go far, Boysie?'

'What, now? Tonight? Or tomorrow?'

'Tomorrow.'

'Don't know. Not yet. Further than I bloody want to, wherever it is.'

'I'll be here, if you want me, when you get back. Well, at the Hammersmith hovel anyway...'

'In your plush pad on the outskirts, eh?'

'If you need me. You will phone, as soon...'

Boysie put his arms round her. 'Of course, Liz. Soon as I get back. But I'll see you later tonight.'

'It's been super. The last few weeks.'

'I know. Sorry about this. You don't know how sorry. See you later then.'

She nodded and reached up to kiss him. Forty-five seconds of controlled eroticism, then, peculiarly embarrassed, Boysie took a deep breath and left the flat.

In a matter of seconds he was back again.

'For crying out loud, Liz, I nearly forgot.'

She came running to the door.

'Someone will be phoning. Bloke called Griffin. Will you tell him that we must meet quickly. Tonight. I'll be cruising up and down Waterloo Bridge at...' He looked at his watch. Seven-ten. Better leave plenty of time. 'Between midnight and one. I must see him, I'll call you to check he's rung. OK?'

'OK. But it's a bit, well, a bit dramatic isn't it? Not like you at all, darling.'

'No,' said Boysie firmly. 'No. It's not like me one itsy little bit.'

CHAPTER TWO

GOLD FLAKE: LONDON

The theatre traffic was beginning its build-up and the rain had started – the pavements of Regent Street littered with plastic-wrapped human parcels trying to flag down empty taxis which hissed past, heading for secret destinations. Liberty's windows were being rigged for the spring tide – dismembered dummies, naked or tissue-pinned, sad and humiliated among haughty little ladies and arty gentlemen. In Oxford Street the plastic parcels and traffic became thicker, the rain more positive – blurring between metronomic strokes of the windscreen wipers. Boysie cursed at having to come the long way. At Marble Arch he swung the E-type into the right-hand lane. Edgware Road. The Lotus House. A shop window bristling with antique armour. Praed Street – sleazy gateway to the West – on the left. Special Briefing on the right, behind a tobacconist's, almost at the frontier where the Edgware Road does its transformation scene into Maida Vale. Keeping Special Briefing far away from the Department HQ was part of Mostyn's long-term decentralization policy, angled to confuse the opposition, and other Government Intelligence Departments. It also served to add a bit of cloak and dagger flavour to life: something which many of the old hands felt had gone from the Department since the war.

The Second-in-Command's silver-grey Bentley was parked across the road from the tobacconist's – too close to the rear of a scarlet Mini. The Mini's back window carried a sticker which said 'Come Home Marples – All is Forgiven'. Boysie brought the Jaguar to within three inches of the Bentley, nearly making a three-car sandwich. He hoped Mostyn wanted to leave in a hurry. There would be a scene. Switching off the engine, Boysie took out a pack of *Benson and Hedges* king-size filters, lit one and eased himself out into the rain. It would ruin the suede, he thought, splashing across the road. The shop front was no credit to its owner, the samples sprayed with a primer of dust. Among them, Boysie noticed several brands which had not been available since his childhood.

Blore, the tobacconist, opened up.

'I've got no *Gold Flake* left,' he said, going through the ritual with a smile of recognition.

'It's not *Gold Flake* I'm after. I want some specials,' parroted Boysie.

'Nice t'see yergain,' said Blore, closing the door behind them and leading the way to the back of the shop. Special Briefing was a small white room furnished with four chairs, a WD folding table, a green WD metal cupboard and an incongruous blue telephone. A solitary 40-watt dangled from the ceiling.

'Someone'll do that recognition pattern one night and a sharp-eared copper'll pull him in on a narcotics charge,' said Boysie.

'Well it won't be me, lad. Sit down, we've got a lot to do.'

Mostyn did not turn from the table, on which a Eumig Mark S projector and slide viewer stood efficiently in readiness. Short, greying curly-hair cut close to the scalp, small hands in repose on a couple of yellow files, Mostyn was a neat, sharp member of the constant ruling classes. The boys who, like *The Brook*, went on for ever – in spite of General Elections and Cabinet changes.

Boysie sat. One of Mostyn's faceless minions materialised from the gloom and stationed himself near the apparatus.

'Slide One,' clipped Mostyn. The picture came up on the screen. 'Know him?'

Boysie's forehead creased, emblazoned with worry. 'I know the face, but...'

'You can't remember the name. I wish you'd keep *with* the government, Boysie. After all, their mistakes are our bread and butter. It's Mr William Penton, Member of Parliament.'

'Westminster whizz-kid.'

'Not the words I would have chosen but they'll do.'

'It's what the *Daily Express* calls him.'

'Yes.' The superior being. 'OK? Red Target L.27 William Francis Penton. Born 1928. Educated Oxford. Sometime lecturer in economics. Extreme leftist leanings. Entered politics through brilliant by-election tactics 1953 at Bettlefield. Ambitious. High tipped as cabinet possibility on formation of last government. Happily the PM took our advice – for a change. Outcry in the popular Press, with whom he has always been at one.'

'Penton Passed Over.'

'That sort of thing. Publicity conscious. Charmer and a traitor. High disposable.

Been ferrying simple stuff for quite a while – trade information mostly. But his name's coming up for an appointment. Can't stave it off this time – that's the reason for the haste. They'll announce it in a matter of days. We've been sitting on this for a long time and I don't want to be forced into toddling to the FO with the dossier at this stage. These new boys think they know it all. Don't want a clash.'

Boysie nodded in understanding and stubbed the last quarter-of-an-inch of the *Benson and Hedges* into the tobacco tin which served as an ashtray. Mostyn continued.

'Other difficulty is that some imbecile has given him access to classified material. No harm done yet, but it advances the urgency somewhat. You want to look him over?'

'It doesn't really matter what I say does it? You'll show the film anyway.'

'Don't be like that, Boysie. I just want you to get some idea of his habits. Might help you to decide on the best way.' Mostyn paused and looked hard at Boysie whose mouth was twitching up severely at the left corner.

'You're a bit on the edgy side, aren't you?' Mostyn sounded calm, a doctor with a nervous pre-operation patient.

'So would you be bloody edgy. You mentioned abroad. That I had to be on a plane in the morning. I mean I presume it's abroad. What's abroad got to do with it?'

'In the fullness of time, dear boy, all things shall be revealed. Just sit back and watch the pretty pictures. You're in the most expensive seats.'

'Double feature. Flavour-of-the-Month – gore,' muttered Boysie.

Mostyn nodded towards the shadow hovering at his elbow, Boysie glanced up. The man was typical of the many servile seneschals Mostyn seemed to have eternally on call for Records or the GIR. He was dressed, Boysie noted, in the livery of upper bracket Civil Service – the striped pants and black jacket giving the man a normality which was almost sinister. The face meant nothing. As Mostyn's PA, Boysie had probably seen him before, but none of the 2 I/C's errand boys had faces one remembered. To Boysie, one of the unnerving things about the past six months had been the revelation that Democracy was still only a pious hope: that the Foreign Office, Home Office and their various satellite departments controlled a network of ruthless intrigue which made the old OGPU look curiously like a clerical gossip society. Behind the white collars and under the bowler hats of ticky-tacky men like this assistant, there lurked a deep particular political nastiness.

The Eumig whirred, and William Penton – trapped on inflammable 8mm – went through his paces. The film was like every other identification film Boysie had ever seen. The IFU, it was well known, employed numerous young men who had failed to make the grade in the *avant-guarde* world of art pictures, hence the odd shots which picked up Penton's sturdy figure charging through shopping crowds, and his face framed between the fingers of some unidentified woman. Boysie sat still and pretended to concentrate. Long ago he had learned the art of assimilating the facts which Griffin would need, discarding the dross, looking interested and making the kind of comments most likely to lead Mostyn into thinking that 'L' was a true professional and proud of his art. The film came to an end and the 40-watt clicked on again.

'Well, at least you'll recognise him won't you?'

'Where do I make contact?' Boysie wondered if he was sounding suspiciously efficient.

'Ah!' Mostyn opened the uppermost yellow folder on which his hands had been resting. Boysie caught a glimpse of airline tickets.

'Friend Penton goes out of the country twice a year.' Mostyn sounded unduly lazy. 'He's a man of habit. Not the safest attribute to a subversive operative. Always goes to the same place – we think he meets a contact there. We know he has a numbered bank account.'

'Switzerland?' said Boysie with what looked like splendid mental agility. He had, in fact taken in the squat winged arrow symbol of Swissair on the tickets.

'Right on the noddle, Boysie. You're a bright lad. Locarno, on Lake Maggiore in the Canton of Tessin – Ticino if you're a local and speak Italian. Know it?'

'Only from the posters.'

'*Das Tessin die Sonnenstube der Schweiz,*' Mostyn's accent was beyond reproach.

'Yes, it would be,' said Boysie, trying to look knowledgeable.

'Always stays at the *Palmira.* Classy. *Sociéte Gastronomique* and all that. Left this evening, due back in ten days.' Mostyn's smile was that of a bookmaker when all the outsiders have come up. 'It would be better for all concerned if he did not return.'

'Come to happy yodelling Switzerland and end up with an alpenstock in the mush.'

'That's what I like about you, Boysie. Your finesse. You're never frightened to show the characteristics of your vile peasant forbears.' He flicked through the file. 'No time to give you a cover. You're booked in at the *Palmira* in your own name. Just a jolly get away person. Tried to make it easy and fiddle you on to a Zürich flight but no can do. Best we can manage is London–Basle. You go on by train. Itinerary.' He passed over the typewritten schedule, sliding a silken finger down the column of times and reference numbers as he talked. 'Swissair flight SR 115 tomorrow at 08.40. Prop aircraft I'm afraid, so you don't get in until 11.00. Leave Basle by train at 12.41 – the BEA – Swissair Terminal's right next to the railway station. Get into Locarno around 17.30 – one change, at Bellinzona. Then you're on your own. Better stay on a couple of days after the accident. If you need it we can always provide you with a recall telegram – sister ill or something. If you need it. OK?'

'OK,' said Boysie without much enthusiasm. His mind pushed forward. He had to get hold of Griffin tonight.

'There's no need for me to tell you that we don't want any fuss with the locals. Just remember it's Switzerland. Useful neutral ground for everyone.'

'Can I go now.'

Mostyn sighed. 'Old son,' he said with immense patience, 'this is your first for two years. Your cover was shattered then. Remember?'

Boysie remembered. There was an unpleasant salty taste coming into his mouth with the normal saliva.

'It would be better for your peace of mind if you spent a little time familiarising yourself with the known opposition along the ground that you're going to cover. If you see any of them, or if you are given any reason to think that you've been detected, move like an overdose of cascara.'

'Rate of knots,' said Boysie, knowing that the faintest whiff of the opposition would probably send him scurrying to ground like a rabbit at the business end of a twelve bore.

'Everything's here,' Mostyn slid the oblong, slim air and rail tickets towards Boysie. 'Economy and 2nd class I'm afraid but the hotel's good. And you can have as long as you like to study this.' He indicated the other yellow folder. 'Names, photographs, the lot. Right up to date. Get as much into your head as possible. My friend will stay with you until you're finished. He takes it back to Records. Then the usual drill. There's a storekeeper on duty in the Armoury and the night clerk will be at Accounts – usual overseas subsistence, I've made it out for a fortnight. The docket is with the tickets.'

Boysie felt the flick coming back in the left side of his mouth. It would look odd if he did not spend at least an hour looking at the file. Then he would have to go HQ and draw his armaments and cash. From the beginning Mostyn had been worried about Boysie being armed, and only allowed him an official weapon when operational. Elizabeth was waiting at the flat. Lord knew where Griffin was. One thing was certain, William Penton was in Locarno and as good as dead. But who the hell was going to kill him?

'Your contact system will be standard. Not going to have you messing about with ciphers. Telephone or cable using a sub-text and try not to make it too obvious, old boy. Please. You can be Roger and I'll be Uncle as usual. During office hours try me through the Bayswater house. You know the number don't you?' Patronising.

'58367.'

'Good. Use the pay telephone or phone from bars. Not the hotel.'

'I know the drill.'

'Good luck, laddie. They tell me that the *Lago Maggiore* is at its best in the spring.' Mostyn was at the door.

'Go and have a funny gallop.' But the Second-in-Command had gone.

Boysie lit a cigarette and opened the folder.

'Would you mind very much walking out here and shifting that four-wheeled sex-symbol of yours, chum.' Mostyn was back, suppressing fury. 'I would like to drive by car to HQ.'

'Do you mean the Jag? Oh dear. Someone blocked your exit?' said Boysie, all innocence.

Five minutes later, Boysie returned to the Swiss file – Mostyn's friend sitting placidly in a corner of the room trying to be unobtrusive. The file was deftly thorough: three pages of neat précis giving a rundown on relations between the Department and the Swiss Authorities, and reminders of the country's value as a posting house and pay-off station. The remainder of the file contained all known details of opposition forces based in Switzerland. Boysie riffled through the pages, pausing for an occasional look at photographs.

'A right bunch of horror comics this lot,' he said aloud.

'You spoke, sir?' said striped pants.

'I did,' said Boysie with friendly smoothness. 'It is something I find myself doing.' He began reading – more to pass the time than to provide himself with information.

Thirty-eight minutes tracked their way round the slim gold Certina on Boysie's left wrist before the telephone made a sound akin to that of 'Whoopee Cushion'. Striped pants did a catspring to the table.

''Allo!' He said into the mouthpiece. His disguised voice, thought Boysie. The voice returned to normal for the next sentences. 'Yes, sir, he's still here.' Then to Boysie, 'Number Two on the line for you, sir.'

Boysie took the phone. 'L,' he said, sounding very competent.

'How goes it, Boysie?'

'I'm just about finished.'

'Good. Nip up to my office would you – when you've finished with Arms. I'll wait for you.'

'Nothing wrong?' Boysie's gut was beginning to flutter.

'Just one little point we've got to clear up before you leave.'

'It won't take long will it?'

'Shouldn't think so. Hop over here, there's a good chap.'

The line went dead and another piece was added to the anxious jigsaw which crumbled and reformed through Boysie's nervous system. Whenever Mostyn did the unexpected, Boysie began imagining the game was up.

The rain had stopped and the Mini had gone leaving the E-type a lonely white success story by the edge of the kerb.

'You could perhaps give me a lift back to HQ.' The faceless one clutched the yellow folder.

'Awfully sorry. No room. Car's stuffed full of gear,' lied Boysie with no regrets.

The assistant was put out. 'Oh.' He might just as well have said, 'Oh well, if that's your attitude.'

'Sorry. I'd better be going.'

'Yes, sir. I'll get the tube.'

'That's it. Be there in no time.'

Boysie routed himself to HQ via Park Lane, Grosvenor Place and Victoria. The telephone call took him only a couple of minutes. Liz obviously did not want to chat. Griffin had phoned and would be there. Griffin would do it, he was sure of that. Griffin would have to do it, even if it meant more money than the old days. It should have been a relief to know that he could at least get hold of Griffin: that he would see him tonight. But as fast as one tic of concern vanished another took its place.

'See you later, darling,' he said to Elizabeth. Elizabeth did not answer. 'Bye-bye, Boysie.' Was all she said. 'Oh, hell,' moaned Boysie, feeling suddenly tired. 'If it's not one bleedin' thing it's another. I never should have joined.' He turned into Whitehall. 'Never should have bloody joined.'

CHAPTER THREE

PINK *AU PAIR*

Snake-Hips was on duty in Reception when Mostyn got back to HQ. Snake-hips was an ash-blonde with a fantastic walk. Men swore they could actually hear the sigh of her thighs brushing each other as she passed by. The rotary cycle of her trunk would have made an experienced belly-dancer turn green.

'Chief's in, sir. Would like to see you immediately.' She looked up from the copy of *Marie Clare* which she had been giving a perfunctory casing under the gold-shaded desk lamp.

'Been waiting long?' Mostyn liked to know these things.

'Only just come in, sir. Seemed a little out of sorts.'

Blast, thought Mostyn. He nodded and stepped into the lift.

The Chief was in full evening dress – with decorations. His desk was clear, except for the eternal bottle of *Chivas Regal*, two glasses (one full), a *Palma Supreme* burning away in the heavy brass ashtray, and a thick pink file which lay ominously abaft the whisky bottle.

'Have a drink,' ordered the Chief, already pouring as Mostyn entered the room. 'And sit down.'

Mostyn sat and said nothing.

'Don't usually discuss your special operations, Number Two. Your blasted business. Ought to alert you on this one though. Might be able to help. Perishin' SB got me out of the Israeli Embassy.'

'Special Branch?'

'Right in the middle of dinner. Best *Schalete* I've ever tasted. One bleedin' mouthful that's all I got – after a wonderful steak.'

'Kosher, of course.'

'Don't be a fool, Number Two. Anyway, SB's showin' the pallid hand of friendship. Marvellous. No co-operation from them year in and year out except when they want something done. Said to the PM only last week – at the workin' dinner – I'd be puttin' in a complaint. Told 'im straight. Seen this before?' He pushed the pink file across the desk. Pink was the colour for 'Pending.

Classified'. The tag bore two words, *'Au Pair'*. Mostyn pulled it towards him and opened it.

'It's one of ours isn't it? Can't say I've seen it before.'

'No. Nor would you. I've been sittin' on it, Keepin' a watching brief as you might say. Har-har.'

Christ, thought Mostyn, I hope he doesn't do that sort of thing too often. When figureheads start actually working things can get snarled silly.

'You got this Penton business sown up?' the Chief's question was unexpected. Mostyn felt less easy than he had done all day. The pause was a shade too long.

'Sorry to ask.' Said the Chief with a shimmer of sarcasm. 'Your bloke on to him? On to Penton?'

'It's being taken care of.' Mostyn was careful. The Chief rarely talked openly about the policy of 'Kill' assignments, even though the whole idea had first germinated inside that whisky and grog-soaked, sea-fevered old mind.

'The word is that Penton's gone to Switzerland,' said the Chief.

'Yes.'

'Lo-bloody-carno.'

58

'Yes, sir.' This was getting serious. The Chief obviously had more of a finger on the pulse than Mostyn gave him credit for.

'Fred-bloody-Karno,' said the Chief thinking it was no end of a joke. 'Your man goin' there, Number Two?' Again there was a pause. The Old Boy was in a needling humour which Mostyn resented. If anyone was supposed to needle people it was Mostyn and he did not take kindly to the same treatment. The Chief spoke again.

'It's all right. I've got to know. To do with this.' He indicated the pink file.

'Our regular man is indisposed I'm afraid.'

'Indisposed?'

'A heavy head cold.'

The Chief gurgled. 'Thumpin' virgins' knickers' man, what's the Department coming to? Off duty with a heavy cold. Castrated eyeballs!'

'He really is most unwell. "L's" taken over.'

'Oh has he?' The words were uttered (the only word for it) with what writers for women's magazines call scorn. Mostyn felt the ugly clammy hand of disaster fumbling around the back of his neck. It was starting, he thought. The ridiculous nervous grind which overtook him when Boysie was

59

in the field.

'You've always shown great confidence in "L", sir.'

'Yes.' The Chief switched tactics. 'I see we've only got one Rover in Switzerland. Where's he?'

'Schaffhausen, on a rather delicate financial deal.'

'A pay-off. Say what you mean, Number Two.'

'A pay-off. Anyway, he's more of an intellectual than a...'

'Heavy. Yes. You may need someone else to look round Lo-bloody-carno though. Someone other than "L". Don't know. Still, you'd better pass all this on to "L". Don't want him goin' in blind. Have another drink and listen.' The glasses were refilled and the Chief talked. As he talked, Mostyn fell deeper and deeper into a state of misery. He was sending Boysie into an area crawling with unpleasant possibilities.

Departmental policy dictated that operatives being armed for the field should be issued with weapons originating from the country to which they were being deployed. Boysie's prize for this trip was the snug Neuhausen SP47/8. It took him only a few minutes to be initiated. Boysie knew the Browning HP35 pretty well, and when you are familiar with the HP35 you cannot go far wrong with the SP47/8.

Boysie was carrying the weapon, patent holster, box of cartridges and spare magazine as he crossed the empty outer office which led to Mostyn's inner sanctum. His nerves were a little calmer. Logic told him the Armoury would not have issued a weapon if anything affected his future – or past – with the Department.

'Enter, old Boysie.' Mostyn all chummy again. The smile on the face of the tiger. Warning signals bleeping through Boysie's system.

'Drink?'

'No thanks.' Boysie playing it cagey. Mostyn took a deep breath and opened his mouth as though to speak, then stopped. Boysie sat down and Mostyn went through the mouth-opening routine again. This time words came out.

'Boysie, old lad.' He was using the *crème fouettée* voice. 'There seems to be a bit of opposition activity in the target area. Sure you won't have a drink?' Boysie shook his head. He knew the 2 I/C's little game. Mostyn continued. 'Nothing to do with the "kill" you understand, but the Chief is most anxious that you should be told. Just so that you can keep your eyes and ears open, that sort of thing.'

'Oh, yes,' said Boysie, unconvinced. A pink folder marked *'Au Pair'* lay on the desk between them.

'Put you in the picture then.'

'Vistavision, colour with stereo.' Boysie was getting daring. Mostyn looked at him as though trying to make up his mind whether to use branding irons or the bastinado. Eventually he compromised and smiled.

'You know what a flap the Home Office gets into over missing aliens?' He paused long enough for Boysie to nod. 'There's a constant link with Interpol and the Special Branch, but did you know that every year roughly 100 *au pair* girls go missing over here? Usually turn up again, admitted. Bit frightened. Some of them taken suddenly pregnant.' Mostyn was leaning back doing his headmaster act. Boysie began to worry again. There had been that nice Norwegian girl. What was her name? Hedda something. Gabler? No, that was old Ibsen. Anyway he hadn't seen her for a year. 'It seems,' said Mostyn, all pear drops, 'that we are interested in fifteen *au pair* girls who've gone

62

AWOL from the London area over the past two years. Mostly German, two Swedish, one Swiss. Don't ask me why, but the SB thinks we ought to show an interest – they don't give much away you know.'

'Fifteen *au pair* girls? Could have formed an international rugger team?'

'Let's not be flippant, son. None of them have subversive or police records. No friendship links. No link at all, except in the manner of their disappearance. All got decent backgrounds, all come to work in respectable homes here. Pattern's the same for the lot. Girl stays about six months. Perfect treasure until one morning the lady of the house wakes up and her little foreign helper has gone. No explanations. Nothing. Madam gets in touch with the agency – all agencies clean as detergents in case you were thinking of asking.'

'I wasn't.'

'Agencies get in touch with the girl's parents and, hooray, all is well. They've had a cable from their darling daughter saying she is unhappy and on her way home. Even give the flight number or train time. But *jeune fille* is not on the plane, or train. And that's the last that's heard.'

'They take their stuff?'

'Clothes? Yes, all the gear goes with them. Interpol's had a trace on the whole caboodle – last one hopped it about six weeks ago – but, so far, nothing. That is until ten days ago. An unconfirmed identification in Bellinzona – near where you're off to.' Mostyn leant across the desk and looked hard into Boysie's eyes in the approved manner of one in authority. 'The identification was made positive yesterday afternoon. The girl was pulled out of the lake. Drowned. It's definite. She's one of the fifteen. Karen Schport. Mother's a widow, remarried a RAF Wing Commander ten years ago. Stationed in West Berlin.'

The Second-in-Command flipped the file open. Each girl had a page to herself – the standard record form with a 2½ inch by 1¾ inch photograph in the top right-hand corner. Any one of them could have made the girlie glossies. They were numbered one to fourteen. The fifteenth had been detached from the file. Mostyn tossed it on to the desk. It spun on the polished surface and ended in front of Boysie, sideways on. Boysie picked it up. Karen Schport. Age 23 years. Height 5 feet 6 inches. Weight 119 lbs. The eyes looked up at him from the photograph. Passport-type eyes which told you nothing. A teletype report was stapled to the form. The body had been recovered from the landing stage at Brissago on Lake Maggiore. Death by drowning not more than twenty-four hours previously. The report was horribly thorough. After the medical description – which jiggled Boysie's stomach – came the personal effects. Light blue all wool day dress with *Lancetti* label. Check cotton bra and pants (no maker's label. Pending enquiry). No stockings. No shoes. One silver wrist chain with attached silver medallion (diameter 2.8 centimetres). Design: winged horse with neck and head of eagle on both faces. Boysie looked up from the file.

'What the hell's it…'

'Got to do with us? I told you, Boysie, you know as much as I do. The SB play it right off the tits. Alerted the Chief some time ago and said they had reason to believe the opposition were in on it.'

'Had reason to believe. Pompous sods.'

'Agreed, old fruit. But if Redland have got a finger in the pie then that part of the world could be warmish and you wouldn't want us to send you out without any warning, would you?'

Boysie looked disgruntled.

'Tell you what,' said Mostyn, 'The Chief merely wants you to keep your peepers open for any of the flown birds. We may also ask you to bring back some of the girl's belongings.'

'She's got damn all poor kid. Dress, pair of drawers, a bra and a bracelet.'

'Ah yes, but it would make a nice little cover for the local authorities wouldn't it? Reason for you being there at all. This is only a possible side issue. Your job's to get friend Penton. Go get 'im, boy.' Mostyn sounded calm. Inside he knew that sending Boysie into a warm zone was like popping an aerosol can into a lighted oven. You were bound to get some reaction. 'Just be prepared. Proper boy scout stuff, eh?'

'Can I go now?' Boysie was still fretting about Griffin and Elizabeth.

'You're in a terrible hurry tonight. Nest getting cold or something?'

'Now look here...'

'Sir.' A razor blade through balsa. Boysie deflated. With Mostyn you just could not win.

'I think,' said Mostyn, thirty seconds later, 'that you'd better sit down and commit the young ladies' physogs to memory. Be on the safe side.' He got up and began to walk slowly towards the door. 'Turn the light out when you're finished and hand in the file to little asp-arse in Reception. I'll tell her you'll be an hour or so. After tonight you'll be a walking mine of information won't you? Our expert on the Swiss area and the *au pair* scandal. Go to it, Boysie.' He shut the door. It opened again a second later. 'Have a good trip, Boysie,' said Mostyn without a smile, 'fix 'im up, won't you. Nice and peaceful. And beware of the girls—

Fifteen au pair girls out courting
One took the final plunge
And then there were fourteen.

Rather good what? Bye, bye.'
  Boysie, a man who hated violence, could have killed cheerfully.

It was ten minutes past midnight when Boysie started his second circuit of Waterloo Bridge, heading south. Griffin was ambling idly along the pavement, walking against the traffic. He got into the passenger seat with a lot of grimaces and a certain amount of pain noises, and Boysie headed the car towards Waterloo Station and the all night buffet.
  They drank their murky sweet tea in

silence, giving each other sly glances across the plastic-topped table which they were forced to share with a middle-aged couple who had ceased speaking, on a day's shopping, at about five in the afternoon. Griffin looked more prosperous than Boysie remembered him. His clothes were fresher and he seemed to have given up the hideous painted ties. The couple eventually left.

'It's been a long time Mr Griffin,' said Boysie.

'Yes, guv'nor, ad I shoubent be 'ere dow by rights. God a filthy cold id de head.'

Boysie felt as though he was falling through the chair, though he could not put his finger on the reason.

'Seasonable,' he said brightly.

'Ah,' said Griffin without much pleasure. 'Whad cad I do for you den, Mr Oakes? Bust ward you first dad de price is ub. Whad wid be overheads and all.'

'Oh that'll be all right,' said Boysie with some relief. 'They say that southern Switzerland is very pleasant at this time of year.'

Griffin perked up and began to look happy. The deal was obviously going to be on.

Boysie got back to the flat around 1.30.

There was a note on the bedside table. *I hate goodbyes. Call me when you get back. All love and thanks. Elizabeth.*

CHAPTER FOUR

BROWN DWARF: BASLE

After the nightmare of flying from London to Basle, Boysie was unprepared for the body-blow waiting for him on Track 10 of the SBB Station at Basle.

He was not actually on the aircraft, but there was that same old feeling of moral, physical and mental disintegration as the two grumbling Pratt and Whitneys increased the airscrew revolutions, and the fat Convair Metropolitan sloped off down runway seven, finally shaking the ground from its wheels to go throbbing into the air.

For over two hours, Boysie sat (refusing the breakfast of coffee, rolls, jam and foil-wrapped Gruyère) with hearing stretched to the full limit, listening for the slightest change in pitch or timing of the motors. Even the most minute air-pocket bumps were registered, by his body, with a surging fear. At one point – shortly after take-off – as an act of bravado, he opened the *Daily*

Express only to find himself staring at a half-page advertisement for BOAC's VC 10 service. A knowing blonde sultered from the page. Beneath, the caption read *There's always time for a new experience.*

'Oh gawd,' groaned Boysie, 'do me a favour.' He closed his eyes, opening them again to view something more to his fancy. Across the aisle a slim girl was stretched lazily in her seat, the hemline of her white and lime Courreges suit riding high and hopefully up a pair of long, provocative legs. One elbow was poised on the arm-rest, a hand cupping her chin, fingers lying smoothly up what looked to be a fine jaw line. The profile was bold, almost classic – not beautiful, for the nostrils flared too much, and the eyes were a shade large to give complete balance to the features. Her eyebrows were plucked and shaped in a professional dark curve, contrasting with rust-coloured hair falling full to the nape of the neck, groomed with a casual elegance. She also refused the breakfast, but in a vague, distant manner which betokened one surrounded by an aura of preoccupation.

The cautionary tocsin began to boom away in Boysie's skull. Something about her. One by one, his brain thumbed through the photographs of the fourteen *au pair* girls. Negative. The rusty-haired girl was reaching into her handbag for cigarettes. Automatically, like a sharp waiter, Boysie had his lighter – the silver Windmaster engraved with the ad-like BO initials – gripped between thumb and first two fingers. He reached out across the aisle, pushing down the plunger. She drew on the cigarette and half-smiled thanks. The large dark eyes looked full into his, but he knew they saw nothing. Behind them, Boysie sensed grief – some spaniel quality. The handbag was still open on her lap, one corner of a passport peering from the debris of feminine requisites. British. She was certainly not one of the *au pairs*. The opposition file? Boysie carefully thought back to the previous evening. The Swiss file had contained only two women. No possible resemblance. Yet there was something about the girl. Connected with the present situation. The problem weaved around for the remainder of the journey – the warp in the weft of terror 30,000 feet above the earth at a steady 289 m.p.h.

The landing pattern at Mulhouse-Basle Airport – is intricate. Incoming aircraft lock-on to the Mulhouse Locator Beacon at

25,000 feet – the beacon pulsing out its call sign MN on 335.5 Kc/s – and fly a long oval 'race-course' pattern, reducing height, when cleared, until the final circuit is made and the aircraft whistles down on to the mile and a half stretch of main runway. There was a lot of cloud. The let-down – with its continual turns at the opposite ends of the race-course – was bumpy. Boysie, always at his worst when flying in cloud, was a damp rag of sweat by the time the Metropolitan's wheels juddered on to the concrete. Customs were courteous, the short bus ride into Basle uneventful. At last, Boysie walked out of the air terminal building and dumped the old tan *Revelation* on the pavement. His ears were bombarded by the clank and ting of Basle's legendary trams which swarm around the Centralbahn-platz.

Boysie looked about him, taking in the conservative Schweizerhof nestling next to a Torquay-style Royal Victoria National. It was noon and traffic swamped the square. The girl disappeared into the crowd with a porter wrapped round her luggage. Boysie felt a twitch of regret. He loathed being alone – out on a limb. And this limb could turn out to be very unshapely. In the old days he had always got the assignments over as quickly as possible, and when he was on the courier work he invariably tried to make some temporary friend – not hard when you had the looks and bearing of Boysie. He shrugged. The train was due out in forty minutes. Picking up the suitcase he ambled into the dark cavern of the SSB Bahnof, heading for his first really big shock of the day.

The 12.41 was waiting in Track 10, a spotless giant which would whisk them across Switzerland, through the great St Gotthard and down to the shores of Lake Maggiore – a vast, mountain-fringed pool bisected by the Italian frontier. Standard 2nd Class coaches on Swiss Federal Railways are built on an open plan system. Leather covered bench seats, for two, run back to back on either side of narrow aisle, making six small compartments – accommodating four people facing each other in pairs – on each side of the car. Boysie chose a car well forward containing only half-a-dozen passengers. The two open compartments to left and right just inside the sliding door – which connected with the narrow entrance lobby and lavatory – were empty. Boysie stowed his suitcase on the rack, went into the lobby and climbed down on to the platform, intent on watching the changing hubbub which marks the departure of any long-distance Continental express. There was a smell of coffee in the air. Boysie was beginning to feel hungry – the nervous exhaustion caused by flying was beginning to wear off. He lit a cigarette – the seventh since landing – and was contemplating a stroll down to the diesel locomotive when the jolt came. Glancing up the train he saw Kadjawaji.

It was like being hit suddenly, and low. Boysie felt a nasty elevator sensation in his guts. Kadjawaji's name had not been on the Swiss file, but his photograph and description appeared on all the Department's Classified 'Danger' lists. Boysie had never seen him in the flesh, but recognition was easy. For one thing Kadjawaji had been born in Java – brown skin the colour of three-quarter black coffee – for another, Kadjawaji was a dwarf. He was also one of the opposition's front line weapons, rarely used but always lethal. A shrewd and ruthless operator, Kadjawaji had originally been an officer under the legendary Tan Malakka and, in spite of his size, proved so effective that the authorities had brought him to Moscow for special training. Since then the record was impressive. He worked – in a circus – in West Germany for four years without being detected, and subversive activity by him had accounted for the disruption of four network controls. In East Berlin he was known to have personally murdered ten senior operatives. Now, too easily identified in the West, his work was confined to very quick sorties, usually the organisation of subversive groups or – Boysie had to face – the same kind of job which he was supposed to carry out.

Kadjawaji came bustling down the platform. The neat grey suit, grey shirt and blue silk tie would have looked smart on a fourth-form schoolboy. The short legs moved rapidly, as though his stature dictated the use of great energy; his head, grotesquely out of proportion nodding from side to side in rhythm with the chubby protruding buttocks. The face set in a permanent snarl – as though he regarded all his fellow men with contempt. Yet it was a face marked by determination – the mania of a deformed and tiny man to be all powerful. He looked, and was, vicious.

The sudden appearance of Kadjawaji, his reputation, and the possible repercussions, made Boysie shudder. He was back up the steps and into his seat – one hand held slyly across his face – with the agility of a mountain goat. Boysie was terrified. One of the nightmares which took hold of him at regular intervals was based on circumstances like this – being alone in the field and meeting one of Redland's top boys. For Boysie knew, to his cost, that the opposition, however misguidedly, believed him to be one of Special Security's supermen. He waited, heart going like a set of bongos and a nasty taste filtering into the back of his mouth. His free hand slid to the hip pocket of his slacks. The Neuhausen had been left, locked way in a drawer at the Chesham Place flat – Griffin was doing the work so what would Boysie do with a dirty great pistol? But it was a comfort to feel the butt of his small unofficial weapon ('a toy' Mostyn would have called it) the Sauer & Sohn 1A adapted for .22 ammunition which lay firm in the patent holster above the right cheek of his bottom. Boysie was facing down the car. The sliding door to his right was half-open and he could now hear someone being helped up into the lobby behind him. Footsteps, and Kadjawaji passed slowly between the seats without a glance in Boysie's direction. The dwarf moved right down to the far end of the car. A passenger spoke in German.

'Shall I put your case on the rack?'

'*Danke.*' Disgruntled and uncivil. A piping voice which would easily grate on the nerves. Boysie's nerves were already more than grated. Triple shredded. He tried to rationalise the situation. There was always the chance that the sub-sized killer would not even recognise him. Boysie glumly accepted that this was unlikely. Kadjawaji was Moscow-trained. The situation was ridiculous. Two of the major powers' top trigger men both in the same coach of a Swiss express with practically five hours' travelling ahead. Presumably the dwarf would use the lavatory at his end of the car, but the restaurant car lay in Boysie's direction. Perhaps he had brought sand-wiches. Little cucumber sandwiches, thought Boysie. Oh hell, it was all Mostyn's fault anyway. Even if he managed to escape any action by Kadjawaji he would have to report the dwarf's presence. In those circumstances Mostyn would expect him to move in with a quick kill, then get out again – fast. But Griffin could not possibly arrive in Locarno until late evening. It would take until tomorrow night at the earliest. And what the hell was this wretched midget doing heading down to Locarno anyway? The *au pair* girls? Perhaps he was going to organise a variety show, *Coal Black and the fourteen dollies.*

Mostyn had told him to move like an overdose of cascara if he spotted any heavy opposition on the ground. He felt as though he had already taken a large glassful of the stuff anyway. The train gave a jolt. They were sliding out of the station. Off to sunny Ticino. A white-coated steward passed down the car banging a little triangle to call diners to the first lunch. The other three seats in Boysie's section were still empty. At least his luck was holding there. He shifted across to the opposite seat so that his back would be towards the dwarf should the little fellow decide to eat. Boysie picked up his now crumpled and grubby copy of the *Express,* opened it, and pretended to become immersed in a somewhat spectacular divorce case. Three men and a woman went by, heading for the chow wagon. Then Isosceles with his triangle. Last, the unmistakable short footsteps of the dwarf. The door slid shut and Boysie relaxed. Kadjawaji would be in the restaurant car for at least an hour. It would be best to move forward. But first, nature had to be appeased. He got up and opened the door, stepping through and close it behind him. Looking down the short, narrow passage and across the lobby he noticed that the other connecting door was also closed. It was as he put his arm forward towards the lavatory door that he realised something was wrong – the rushing noise of air and the strong draught. The outer door, to his left, was open, swung inwards and resting against the wall. The train gathered speed and began to sway. The open door would be a danger to passengers passing through. Boysie stepped across, feeling boy scoutish, and put his left hand on the edge of the door to swing it shut. Suddenly he experienced that terrible crawling of the skin which comes a second before danger strikes. He half-turned, but his warning had been too late. The dwarf sprang forward from the other side of the lobby. The tiny hands fastened themselves around Boysie's right ankle. He tried to kick, but the force of the pull was so sharp and unexpected that all sense of balance went. Boysie caught a glimpse of green, a wooden building, white, a signal gantry – all flicking past the open door. Then he was sprawling outwards still clutching at the door's edge. In a second his momentum would carry him right through the opening, pulling the door with him in a curve. His hands would be crushed between door and jamb, and he would go shrieking away, whipped from the train like a chocolate wrapping thrown by a child. The automatic action of self preservation took charge. The wind was already banging at his legs, pulling his body out of the doorway. Boysie let go of the door and grabbed outwards. His arms made contact with the long curved handrail which ran down the outside of the coach. Boysie hung on. His body swung outwards and thudded painfully against the side of the coach. He could hardly breathe and the roar of air was like the rush of some hideous whirlwind. He pulled desperately against the heavy weight of air which pressed him against the coach. His arms were slowly being wrenched from their sockets. Another pull and he was able to move his body forward, his right foot finding a hold on the step. As it did so, the dwarf appeared in the doorway, clinging unsteadily to the inside, smiling and looking back along the train in the hope of seeing Boysie's body splayed out on the track. The smile turned to a leer of surprise. He shouted something and reached clumsily into his inside pocket. Boysie heaved again. The foothold was strong. Kadjawaji lifted his right hand, still hanging on to the inside of the door with his left. The right hand held what looked to be an air pistol. Boysie made a final effort and pulled himself up straight beside the doorway, feet on the top step and arms hugging the handrail. The train began to take a left-hand bend, there was the sound of its hee-haw klaxon and then an increased swaying outwards. Boysie had to cling tighter to maintain his position. The dwarf, insecure on the edge of the step, faltered. His right hand, still clutching the weapon, moved across to save himself. The tiny fingers of the left hand scrabbled against the door frame, but all hold had gone. The body arched outwards, then began to turn towards Boysie. Boysie felt Kadjawaji's shoulder bump heavily against his side and saw the face contorted with fear. He turned his head to watch the child-like figure spin and crash into the grass bank a good twelve feet away. It seemed to bounce, roll into a small human ball and bump down the further side of the slope. For a second, Boysie had the strange impression that he had been through all this before. Then he realised that he was thinking of an old movie. This was for real. He pulled himself painfully back into the lobby – still deafened by the rush of air, aching and shaking like a man on his first day off heroin. He closed the door and headed for the lavatory. It was a good half-hour before Boysie could even begin to think normally. The dwarf must have spotted him from the very beginning. 'The black bastard,' said Boysie to the wash basin. 'The little black bastard.' The depression set in. He had not even coped with the midget. It had been pure chance, luck, that had sent Kadjawaji flying off the train. 'Please somebody,' said Boysie quietly, 'please take me home. I'm not up to it. I'm really not up to it.'

There was plenty of room in the restaurant car. Boysie eschewed the food and ordered a large Courvoisier. Then another. After three he felt better. The magnificence of the mountains, the steady warmth in his stomach and the friendliness of the waiters all played a part in his recovery. By the time they reached Andermatt, on the edge of the St Gotthard, Boysie was starting to tell himself that skill had won the fight with the dwarf. On the other side of the St Gotthard the sun was shining and by ths time Boysie

– with the help of two more brandies – had convinced himself that all danger had passed.

'Good old Griffin'll be in Locarno tonight,' thought Boysie. 'Old Griffin'll do the job'n we can all go home. Shuper!'

The spring sun was quite warm when they changed trains in Bellinzona for the last short lap down to Locarno. The little, crowded 'local' pulled in dead on time. Boysie smiled, sniffed the air and allowed a dark happy man, wearing a claret cap inscribed *Hotel Palmira,* to take his case and lead him down to the Ford Station Wagon. There was already one passenger inside – the rust-haired girl from the aeroplane, still sitting wrapped in her thoughts.

Boysie pulled himself together, the brandy was wearing thin in the bloodstream, anxiety nibbling through. But the natural man within sprang into action.

'Hallo,' he said. 'Weren't you on the plane from London this morning?'

She looked at him without recognition. 'Yes. Oh! Yes, you gave me a light.'

Boysie extended a hand. The girl did not move for a moment. It was as though she was not quite sure what to do. Then, waking up to the situation she lifted her hand and brushed his palm with hers.

'Oakes,' said Boysie.

'I beg your pardon?'

'My name. Oakes. Friends call me Boysie.'

Again the feeling that she had not taken it in.

'Oh yes. Whitching. My name's Petronella Whitching.'

The name meant nothing to Boysie, but, once more he felt certain that he should know something about the girl.

The *Palmira* is one of those strange paradoxical continental hotels. Its rating is high and – with places like *Auberge du Père Bis* at Talloires, and *La Côte-d'Or* at Saulieu – is listed in the *Passeport Gastronomique*. It's specialities include *Rognons Flambés* and *Omelette Stephanie*, and from the exterior it looks like any other lush modern luxurious caravanserai which you can see from Miami to Madrid. Its front rises in an impressive display of sweeping balconies, a dazzle of concrete, glass and high gloss. But once past the palms and fish ponds which decorate the entrance you are enmeshed by a décor of golden Second Empire – admittedly, mixed at times by interior decorators with their minds heavily bedded in the twentieth century. Walking up the wide steps to the elegant plate glass doors, Boysie glanced at the array of coloured shields announcing various organisations' faith in the hotel. *The Automobile Club Suisse* was well to the fore, and Boysie smiled to see the blue metal tag which stated that the *Palmira* was a *Bond's Hotel.* The foyer was a blaze of gilt and gee-gaw. A neat receptionist handed out the usual forms. The bellboys ogled Petronella, and a tall grinning concierge bowed decorously – his uniform lapels emblazoned with crossed keys. Boysie immediately christened him St Peter. The white and lime suit showed Petronella's figure to an undoubted advantage. Boysie sidled up to her.

'I wonder if you'd care to dine with me...?' he began.

The same expression of unknowing. 'I'm very tired.' Shaking her head. 'No, I'm sorry.'

'Perhaps some other time?'

'Perhaps.' Only the faintest smile as she was conducted from the desk.

Boysie had to wait for the lift. He felt dirty and untidy. He was dirty and untidy, he knew it by the condescending way the bell-boy kept looking at his shoes. In spite of the impeccable taste with which he had been indoctrinated by the Department, Boysie always managed to get intimidated by hotel officials. 'Bang goes your tip, laddie,' he thought staring back at the bellboy. The lift came down and the doors opened noiselessly. Out stepped Mr William Frances Penton, MP. Deferentially, Boysie moved to one side. Penton swept by without even a gesture of thanks. He was a podgy man. Obviously a 'person' by his assured manner. But not a man to love. The face was overtly conceited, and the patent-leather hair betrayed his proletarian background. Boysie caught himself thinking like Mostyn again. Anyway, it was as relief to know that he felt quite out of sympathy with the target.

The room was a smaller version of the foyer, though the bathroom favoured contemporary epic. Boysie unpacked, bathed and rang down for *Oeufs Aladdin*, half-a-bottle of '57 *Châteaux d'Yquem* and coffee. He ate the poached eggs, on their saffron-flavoured *risotto*, sitting in the room's one easy chair dressed only in his blue Y-fronts, covered with a towelling bath robe, washing down the light meal with two-thirds of the Bordeaux and three cups of coffee. His body ached from the experience of the afternoon. Getting up painfully he changed into his pyjamas and locked the bedroom door. At nine o'clock the white bedside telephone squawked.

'Goldblat.'

'Who?' said Boysie. Perplexed.

'Goldblat.' There was a short stretch of silence. 'That wad de nabe you told be to use, wadn't it?' said Griffin. The head-cold sounded dreadful.

'Oh Lord. Yes. Forgot. Sorry.'

'Well id wad you what told be to use a false nabe,' said Griffin sublimely unsafe.

'Yes.'

'Well I just god id. I'b at de *Muralo* just ub de road frob you.'

'Oh!' said Boysie. This was a new Griffin. The *Muralo* looked almost as plush as the *Palmira*. Griffin used to like sleazy little hideaways.

'Glad you arrived safely,' said Boysie, frigid. 'I rather want to get our business finished as soon as we can manage it.'

'Well id'll hab to waid 'dil tomorrow. I'b bloody tired and de cold's gone to be chest,' wheezed Griffin. 'You come ub and see me in de mornid, Mr Oakes, will yer?'

'Yes.' Unnerved at Griffin's show of spirit. He was usually quite a service fellow.

'Dat's kind ob yer. Meself I wouldn't mind

lettin' id 'ang od a bit. Fancy this place I do.'

'We'll talk about it in the morning.' Boysie trying to recapture the initiative. 'Wait for me at your hotel. All right?'

'That's wad I said I'd do.'

'OK then. Goodnight.'

'Goodnight, Mr Oakes. You comfortable at your place?'

'Very, thank you. Goodnight.' He firmly replaced the receiver. It would be just his luck, he thought, if Griffin started playing up on this one. When they had first come to the arrangement he just got on with it. No fuss. Now, fancy ideas, smart hotels.

'Touch of the bleedin' prima donnas,' said Boysie aloud.

He walked over to the balcony windows, opened them and stepped out into the fresh night air, standing there for a time, smoking and leaning against the rail. Below, the street was bright from the hotel's illuminations, the pavement across the road glistening in the light from tall standards dotted along the lake front. He could see clear round the bay upon which Locarno is built. Across the dark waters of the lake, the mountains took irregular black bites out of a shell-coloured sky. Boysie stiffened. Directly in front of the hotel a large willow mushroomed its tendrils in a wide umbrella which trailed to the pavement, on one side, and the lake on the other. Through a gap in the filigree of branches, Boysie saw two people leaning against the low stone wall which separated the pavement from the lake shore. They were standing close in a confidential huddle. The man was Penton. Now the light caught the girl's hair. She turned and looked back towards the hotel, still talking. The girl with Penton was Petronella Whitching.

CHAPTER FIVE

BLACK LEATHER: LOCARNO

In spite of the mental and physical exhaustion, Boysie's body refused to give itself to sleep. Around two in the morning he got up and smoked a cigarette. This only produced heart palpitations, making matters worse, because he soon became convinced the wretched blood pump was operating up-tempo. Just as consciousness was on the verge of suppression, he sat up with a start – certain the heart had stopped altogether.

Eventually, Boysie got out of bed again and sorted through the stock of medical aids he carried, mixed with the toilet gear, in the green Onyx Travel Kit. Discarding Oblion, Dramamine, Aspirin and Alka Seltzer, he settled for a couple of Weldorm tablets which took him of into a heavy if unnatural, slumber. As the comforting ink of unconsciousness seeped into him, Boysie vowed he would make a determined effort, once back in London, to do something

91

about his physical fitness. If he ever got back to London. Being a country boy, Boysie always took pride in bodily prowess. Not through motives of toughness, but simply because of a built-in desire to feel that he was functioning properly – no matter what bizarre neuroses plagued his mind. The winter with Mostyn had made him flabby.

The Weldorm carried him through until 8.30. He ordered coffee and rolls, shaved and dressed – it was warm enough for his lightweight bought in San Diego. At least the desk job had added nothing to his waist-line. He struck up a couple of postures before the mirror. The colour suited him. Mostyn had called it 'rich sputum green'. Boysie clipped the A1 into its holster and went out to the balcony. The day was bright. Not with the brilliant early sun of summer – which, even at dawn picks up the dregs of the previous day's heat – but a clear wash bringing out the detail, as sharp as a Tessar lens. From the third-floor vantage point, this end of the lake appeared to be entirely surrounded by mountains, making it a lost basin, painted and decorated with brilliant strokes of grey-green, blue and flashing white. Along the shore, colour was height-ened by tufty palm-tops, bursts of blossom and splashes of camellia and mimosa. No wonder, thought Boysie, that the Locarno issue of *Journal des Voyages*, provided by a thoughtful management, called it 'Shangri-La.' A romantic name. A romantic landscape. The bedside telephone made its obscene noise.

'Hallo.'

'Good mornink, Mr Oakes.' It was the cheerful voice of the lanky concierge whom Boysie had christened St Peter.

'I hope you have slept well.'

'Morning.'

'There is a gentleman down here to see you.'

Blast Griffin, thought Boysie. Why the hell hadn't he stayed at his hotel as arranged?

'Ask him to wait. I'll be down in a minute.' He was not going to have Griffin snooping around his room. Chap might get even grander ideas. Want more loot.

The entrance hall at the *Palmira* combines foyer and general public lounge. When Boysie stepped out of the lift there were only half-a-dozen people around – drinking coffee at the ornate Louis XV tables, checking up on the stock market prices, or shielding themselves with the morning papers. Griffin was nowhere to be seen. St Peter smiled broadly behind his desk with the carefully arranged postcards and tourist information, backed by keys and pigeon-holes.

'The gentleman is over there.' He indicated a lone little man sitting by the broad, oblong window looking out on to the street and lake shore. He had the face of a small animal. A rodent of some kind. The movements matched. The voice quick and sharp. He rose as Boysie approached.

'Mr Oakes?' A hand almost quivering in welcome.

'Yes.'

'Gatti. Department of Justice. I have to give you...' He paused, mentally running an invisible finger down his spotless English vocabulary. 'The effects.'

'The effects?' Boysie was on a different wavelength.

'Fraulein Schport. Your people want her effects. I have them for you. That is why you came here is it not?'

'Oh yes.' Boysie readjusted and sat down across the table. On the chair to his left Gatti had placed a neat, square cardboard box. He picked it up with care holding it towards Boysie – a reverence which suggested it contained his favourite aunt's ashes.

'The clothes are in here. Our forensic

laboratory has been over them. Your experts will no doubt also want to take tests.'

Boysie took the box, holding it awkwardly, uncertain what to do. At last he placed it on the table.

'I have a form for you to sign. It is important to show that you have received everything. Had you not better look?'

Boysie nodded and began to fumble with the box lid. 'Didn't really expect you to make contact as quickly as this.' His hand came out of the box. 'Only arrived last night.' He looked to see what he had drawn out – there was a fleeting thought that it was rather like a lucky dip. The grin slipped from his face. He was sitting in the respectable lounge of the best hotel in town holding high above the table a brassière and a pair of unmistakably feminine briefs – flimsy in violent black and flame check. An elderly lady viewed him with distaste through a lorgnette. He glanced towards St Peter's desk. The concierge looked at him with surprise. Boysie hastily stuffed the garments back into the box, fastened down the lid and replaced it on the chair. He smiled. His sheepish smile. Gatti looked solemn.

'I think it's all in order. I trust you,' said Boysie.

'You must be certain. It is a good thing that I am an honest man. Only the clothes are in the box.' His hand darted into pocket and reappeared with a small object wrapped in tissue paper. With the same extreme tenderness he had shown towards the box, the Swiss placed the packet in the centre of the table and carefully unfolded the tissue. The silver chain was about five inches long, the medallion a shade smaller than a penny. It was easily recognisable from the description – a winged horse with the head and neck of an eagle. Not a great work of art, but certainly not mass produced. The lake water did not seem to have done any harm, though there was normal black discoloration round the edges of the engraving.

'Unusual,' said Boysie.

Gatti nodded. 'It is not unpleasant.' He raised his head looking quickly to Boysie's left. Boysie heard a sharp intake of breath behind him. He turned. Petronella Whitching – beautifully on display in white stretch pants and shirt – stood about four paces away. Her large eyes no longer showed the cloudy lethargy Boysie had noticed the day before. Now, she glared down at the silver trinket lying between the two men.

'Good morning,' said Boysie happily.

Three seconds' silence. She turned the full stare of her eyes on to Boysie. The look was of arrogance blended with unconditional hatred. Puzzled, Boysie still tried to maintain his smile. With a slight hiss of disgust, the girl turned away and walked swiftly towards the main doors. Boysie watched her go, still poised, long legs sheathed in white moving with beautiful elegance, back straight and head tilted.

'Who was that?' asked Gatti. Boysie did not hear. He was shuffling through the facts given to him by Mostyn – hastily filed somewhere in the central cortex. Still no answer clicked into position. Boysie was disturbed, his palms dampening. Gatti repeated the question.

'Oh, a girl I met coming over yesterday. No one in particular.'

'She seemed worried.'

'Yes.' The mental probes clutching out in a dozen different directions. 'I think I upset her last night. Away from home. You know how it is.' He spread his hands and hunched his shoulders in the popular conception of a money-lender explaining to a client that times aren't what they were.

'I have been told.' Gatti was stiff. 'Personally I am a happily married man with six children and a house of my own. Will you sign the paper?'

Crushed, Boysie took the official form and scratched out his autograph. Gatti stood up. 'I hope you have a pleasant journey home.'

'Thank you. I'm staying on here for a day or so. There is no urgency about these.'

'No? Well, goodbye, Mr Oakes.' Distaste in his manner. Boysie went with him to the door, then walked back to St Peter's desk – over what seemed to be a mile of choice Persian.

'I'm going to my room. Can you get me the *Muralo* on the telephone.'

'Of course, sir. Anything.'

Boysie gave him that secret look which says, 'You look after me, brother, and your palm will be well oiled – a full lubrication with the folding green'. St Peter nodded his understanding and Boysie made for the lift.

'Oh, sir.' The concierge bustled out from behind his barricade, eager to be of assistance. 'Your friend. He left his parcels.'

'Eh?'

'On the chair, the packages.' St Peter was off across the lounge. He came back grinning and looked as pleased as a retriever depositing a brace of pheasant at his master's feet, the cardboard box and tissue packet held out to Boysie.

'Oh, thank you. Mine actually.' He took the objects and thought he detected a knowing, amused look in St Peter's eyes.

Boysie dumped the cardboard box in the wardrobe, left the bracelet in his pocket and sat on the bed waiting for his call. St Peter got through quickly.

'Could I speak to Mr Goldblat.'

'Mr Goldblat. Room 378. One moment please.'

Griffin came on the line.

'Good morning. It's your old friend.'

'Ah. Good morning. 'Ad a good sleep then?'

'Fine. How about you?' Boysie keeping it formal.

'Me cold seem to 'ave disappeared overnight. Feel swinging. Slept like a bleedin' log.'

'What about dealing with the dead wood then.' Mostyn would have liked that.

'Ah well, sir, let's 'ave a little talk, eh? I seen 'im last night by the way. Walkin' along the front 'ere.'

'I thought you were going to bed last night. Tired.'

'Changed me mind. Decided I'd 'ave a look see. And I saw. Place is better'n Eastbourne. Never been 'ere before.'

'Where are we going to meet?' Boysie brought Griffin back to the problem in hand.

'Well I was just goin' out anyway, guv'nor. 'Ow about an aperitif? There's a nice little place next to me hotel. Went there last night. *Bar Sylveste* right next door. Fancied the name. Reminded me of me old army days. You ever 'ear that song?' Griffin broke into melody. It sounded like the cry of a strangulated hernia:

'That's my brother Sylveste,
'E's got lots of curly 'airs upon 'is chest...'

To his shame, Boysie recalled singing the lyric on many occasions, shoulder to shoulder with fellow sufferers in the backs of innumerable Army trucks.

'Remember it, guv'nor?'

'Can't say I've heard it before,' lied Boysie.

'Oh. Rollickin' song that. *My Brother Sylveste.*'

'Have you been drinking?'

'Not what *you'd* call drinkin', guv'nor. No.'

'And you say this *Bar Sylveste's* all right.'

'The goods.'

'Next to your hotel?'

'Can't miss it.'

'Meet you there in ten minutes.'

''Ave an 'art, guv'nor. Make it twenty. Only just got out of bed.'

Boysie was on his second *Campari* by the time Griffin arrived. The *Bar Sylveste* was nothing out of the ordinary. Just another bar. Boysie sat outside at one of the little round tables watching the world of Locarno go by, and reflecting on Griffin. In the couple of years since they had worked together, Griffin had undergone an unsubtle change. Boysie had always been the undisputed master. It was he who gave the orders, put the finger on the client. Paid the bill. Griffin stayed in the background. A shadow. One who obeyed and did the job – in the most professional way. Now he was spreading himself. Boysie could not help thinking of Mostyn's remark about his successor in the liquidating business– 'Your replacement's got a touch of the 'flu'. Griffin had been bunged up with cold. No. Ridiculous. Mostyn would never have Griffin working for the Department. He was a rougher diamond than Boysie had been. If they were using Griffin they would have given him the treatment. The good food and wine touch. The culture bit.

'En't it smashin' then? That view of the

lake.' Griffin was dressed in flannel slacks (Boysie winced at the 20 inch bottoms and turn-ups) held up with braces over a shirt the colour of dried blood. He wore large, black, rimmed sunglasses and over his shoulder hung a Carena pistol-grip 8mm movie camera and a light-meter.

'What the hell do you think you're got up as?'

'Shh, guv'nor.' Griffin sat down. 'I'll 'ave one of those bitter orange things you're guzzlin', please.'

Boysie swallowed the remainder of his drink and signalled to the waiter.

'*Due Campari Prego*'. Out to impress.

'Yes, sir. Certainly, sir,' said the waiter. Boysie threw a couple of knife-looks in his direction.

'What about this bloody fancy dress?'

'Walls 'ave ears,' said Griffin. The waiter returned flicking the coasters on to the table with the agility of a three-card man. When he had gone Griffin spoke.

'It's the projection of me new image.'

'Your new what?'

'No, I'll level with yer, Mr Oakes. I'm only doin' this one as a favour. 'Cause of the large amount of business you used to put in my way. You still can't manage it yerself then?'

'No,' said Boysie curtly.

'There's some as can and some as can't. Never bothered me death didn't. Funny en't it?'

'Very jocular. What's this about levelling with me?'

'It's like I said. I given it up really. But for you, Mr Oakes. Any time.'

'Why the get-up?'

'What get-up? Oh the gear. Merges better with the background, don't it? Tourist. Read in a book that the ignorant Englishman abroad always wears his braces showing and drinks Guinness.'

'But you're not drinking Guinness. You're drinking *Campari*.'

'Ah, well I'm not that dead ignorant. Am I?'

'Look, if you want to attract attention you're going the right way about it. Tourist? Christ. I do know what I'm talking about you know. I've been trained in these things.'

'You've been trained in the other as well, and you still can't do it. Still 'ave to send for me.'

'If it's a question of him or me I can always...' Boysie brindled. Then, like a small boy who cannot manage an exercise on the horizontal bar, 'It's only the cold thing.

Calculated.' He was fiddling with his tie. 'You look a mess. People will remember you.'

'All right, guv'nor, go and do the bloody job yourself.'

Boysie groaned. After a while he said, 'I'm sorry, Mr Griffin. I didn't want to do this one at all. Bit nervy. You go ahead.'

'Only if you'll save your bloody criticisms until after it's all over. I've always given good service, Mr Oakes. I can give good service this time. I'm a professional. You know that. You trust me. I'll see yer all right.'

Boysie looked hard at the man. In spite of the change of attitude, the awareness to Boysie's need of him, the strange clothes, Griffin was the same old Griffin. His fingernails needed desperate attention. Boysie sighed. 'Go ahead then. But I want this finished as quickly as you can.'

'Ah, now that's the point. You never said nothing' about that back in London.'

'Circumstances change.'

'You said the bloke was down here for ten days. What you said first was "Southern Switzerland is very pleasant at this time of the year". Now what's the point in finishin' it off quick with all this lovely scenery and spring sunshine hangin' about? It'd be

104

murder to go straight back to London.'

Boysie was not going to argue. 'I want it finished. Now. As soon as you can. Right?' He rose with his gorge, half the *Campari* still in his glass. He would show Griffin who was master. The waiter hovered like a buzzard. 'You understand?'

'I understand,' said Griffin unperturbed.

'But do you, guv'nor?'

Boysie paid the bill and left – huffy, very uneasy and still racking his brains about Petronella Whitching. More complications were waiting for him back at the hotel.

A naïve-looking mouse-blonde – cream skirt, sweater and ankle socks – was violently chatting up the receptionist when Boysie returned to the *Palmira*. St Peter, standing near, looking worried, was trying to deal with two pink-rinsed Americans. Boysie was in no mood for standing on ceremony. He had already decided that he would stay in his room – even eat in his room – until Griffin had done the job. He would then catch the first available train back to Basle or Zurich.

'My key, please.' Snapping rudely across the conversation. The girl turned towards Boysie. Her hair was cut short, a straight fringe ending above clear grey eyes in which fear and innocence swirled in equal proportions.

'You're English?' she asked quietly.

'Yes.' St Peter put the key into his hand as the girl took hold of his arm, tugging him gently away from the desk. Loudly she said, 'How absolutely fabulous to see you after all this time. Fancy meeting you here.' The accent was snobby green belt. Possibly Esher, thought Boysie.

'What the devil are you on about?' he asked warily. Those neat lips and toothpaste commercial teeth might become temping.

'Listen.' She spoke rapidly and low. 'What are you doing here? Holiday?'

'Yes.' Boysie sounding as bewildered as he felt.

'I'm taking a terrible chance on you and I don't suppose you'll believe this but it's very important. My name's Lynne Wheater. I'm at *Il Portone...*'

'*Il Portwhateh?*'

'*...one.* Up the lake. The other side of Ascona.' She was terribly nervous. Boysie knew the symptoms. Even speaking softly fear quavered round her vocal chords. She kept giving regular, sharp looks towards the doors.

'It's a finishing school. Famous. You must have... Oh god she's here. I'm in trouble. Please you must get a message to my father. Please, can you remember, Colonel Wheater. Wimbledon 32697. Please. Tell him Lynne's got the amber nine trouble.'

'The amber...'

'Please.' Pleading.

'All right. Don't worry, 32697.'

'Nobody else. Just my father. Don't tell her. They're coming up behind us. What's your name? Quick.'

Boysie thought with unusual speed. 'Oakes. Brian Oakes. Boysie to my friends.' As if by mutual agreement he turned with the girl. Both were tense, as though ready to ward off an attack.

'Ah, there she is. Come along, Lynne.' The accent was barely noticeable. She was short, neat, tidy and obviously a woman of authority. For a second, Boysie experienced another quick flick of recognition which died almost before it took hold. There was something about the face – a distinction around nose and eyes – crowned by perfectly managed hair, thick and reorganised from its natural colour into a bluey cobweb-grey. She wore breeches, black riding boots, like polished ice, and a thin white shirt open at the neck. A single diamond flashed on her right hand which firmly held a riding crop. On the grave side of thirty or not, this was a woman to be considered sensually by any man. She was flanked by two much younger girls. Both blonde, tall and wickedly leggy. Both dressed identically: tight short-shorts of black leather, which cut into their thighs like briefs, and grey shirts. It said a lot for the booted lady that her two lieutenants in no way outshone her. There was an almost aggressive sexiness about the trio as they marched – three abreast – across the foyer towards Boysie and the girl.

'I'm so glad we've found you, Lynne,' said the leader as they came close. The two blondes dropped back slightly. 'You're not going to be silly and make a scene are you? It wouldn't be wise. And it wouldn't be very nice.'

'No Principal.' Lynne was emanating the cowered fear of a trapped animal.

'Introduce me to your friend then, child.' Hurling a gilt-edged smile at Boysie.

'Er, coincidence actually. He's a friend of Daddy's.'

In for a penny, thought Boysie. 'From Esher.' He said with a grin meant to conjure up nice houses, families, commuting dads, and the sound of lawmowers on summer evenings.

'Mr Oakes, our Principal, Doctor Thirel.'

'Klara Thirel,' said Klara Thirel with great charm, extending a hand. Boysie thought she wanted him to kiss it. He shook instead.

'How do you do. Principal?'

'Of *Il Portone*. "The Gateway". You've surely heard of "The Gateway". Hasn't Lynn told you? Or her father?'

'I haven't seen Lynne or Colonel Wheater for some time. Have I, Lynne?' passing the buck.

'No,' said Lynne, stuck.

'Well, your father wouldn't approve of all this, would he, dear? You'd better say goodbye to Mr Oakes and go on with the girls. We'll have a little chat later.'

Lynne's face had gone the colour of marble. She gave a small frightened smile and whispered, 'Goodbye, Mr Oakes. Give Daddy my love if you see him.'

Boysie nodded. The blondes stopped eyeing him up and down as though pricing a horse, and fell in on either side of the girl like military policemen. As they moved away, Boysie could not help feeling that the ingénue Lynne was under arrest.

'I'm sorry about this.' Klara Thirel looked

at him intently, head cocked to one side. 'It's nerves mainly – her first term. Some of them react like this and try to get home on their own. She'll be all right. We've all been homesick at one time or another.'

You can say that again, thought Boysie.

'At one time or another,' repeated Klara Thirel as though reading his mind. 'You don't know of our establishment?'

'I'm afraid not. Remiss of me.'

'Not at all. Why should you. We're quite well known though. *Il Portone* is, I like to pride myself, the most exclusive finishing school in Europe. Maybe we have odd methods, but they work. We specialise in – how can I put it – difficult cases. From the right kind of homes of course. Our results are good. Are you here for long, Mr Oakes?'

'A few days.'

'You must come and see us at work. Come and see Lynne. She didn't say anything to you? About the school? Anything that struck you as odd?'

Boysie played it safe. 'No.' Firm and true blue.

'Well, I'll be in touch.' It was almost an invitation to more than just an open day at the school.

'I'd be most honoured.' Boysie returning

charm for charm.

'And I would personally be delighted to entertain you. There will be an invitation before you leave.' She held out her hand.

'A charming lady,' said St Peter. Boysie sidled over to the desk, his eyes fixed on the retreating flexible figure of Doctor Thirel.

'Tell me more.' A hand reaching for his wallet. St Peter waved away the intention as though to say, 'Not now, but make it good when you leave'.

'There is not much to tell. I believe she is German. Her finishing school is good. Well, you saw those two girls. Phew. The uniform is...'

'A revelation. That was the school uniform?'

St Peter nodded, a Cheshire Cat smile splitting his face like a segment of melon.

'Better than the old gym-slip and bloomers,' Boysie to himself. Aloud. 'What sorts of ages?'

'They have to be over eighteen. I know because an English milord brought his daughter here last year. He offered Doctor Thirel much money, but she would not have her at the school. She was only seventeen. It is very difficult to get into the school.'

'I'll bet,' said Boysie and headed towards

the lift. An evening at Klara Thirel's establishment would be amusing. Girls in black leather shorts wall to wall.

A bucket and mop stood against the wall outside Boysie's door, which was slightly ajar. Chambermaids, he grinned. The cardboard box was on the bed. Bending over it, back to the door, removing the pathetic clothing garment by garment was Petronella Whitching.

'What the blazes!'

She straightened and turned, eyes repeating the look she had given him in the lounge. There was a second's silence, then she sprang, nails reaching for his face. Boysie grabbed her arms and held on, pulling her to him. For a moment he felt a thrust of excitement as her chest was crushed against his. Then, Petronella threw back her head and spat full in his face.

'You bastard,' she hissed. 'Bastard! Bastard! Bastard!'

Boysie was not listening. He had become aware of his right hand round her left wrist. She still struggled. He glanced downwards. On her left wrist, Petronella Whitching wore a single silver chain with a dangling medallion. Engraved on the medallion was a horse's body from which sprouted the neck and head of an eagle. It was the link. He had seen it, yet not seen it, on the plane yesterday. In his pocket was its twin, the bracelet taken from the drowned body of Karen Schport.

'For God's sake, you bloody little maniac, just shut up and tell me what this is all about,' surprised at his own power of command.

Petronella Whitching began to cry.

CHAPTER SIX

SILVER HIPPOGRIFFIN: LOCARNO

Petronella was quiet now. Under control and sitting, beautifully bedraggled, on the bed. Boysie had let the hysteria have its head. Burn itself out. He bent down taking hold of her left wrist, gently but with purpose – like a doctor about to feel the pulse. At the same time he slipped the medallion from his pocket, allowing its tissue wrapping to fall away. The little silver bauble dangled from its chain, bumping against its twin which hung from Petronella's wrist.

'What's it all about then?'

Petronella, sniffing, said nothing.

Boysie gave the medallion a tiny jerk. 'This was taken from the body of a girl called Karen Schport. She was drowned near here. You're wearing an identical medallion. Life's difficult enough for me already. You knew her?'

The girl nodded, lips close together. 'Who are you?' she asked.

'Does it matter?'

'If...' She faltered. 'If you helped to kill her it matters.'

Boysie sighed. 'I'm a Government courier. I came over to collect her clothes. She's been missing for some time. A lot of people have been looking for her. You knew?'

'I knew.'

'Well?' Still nothing. 'Wouldn't it be better to get it all off your...' His eyes lingered below her neckline. 'Better to tell me all about it?'

'Karen Schport was my sister.'

'Your...?'

'Step-sister. My own mother died when I was seven. My father's in the RAF.'

'Whitching's your real name?'

'Yes. We were stationed in Hamburg. Karen's mother was an interpreter. They married ten years ago and we all came back to England. Karen and I went to the same school. Father was posted to Weston-super-Mare. Then we moved to London. Karen was...' Trying to lock back the tears again. 'I'd always wanted a sister. Silly, silly. But we got on so well. Then father was posted back to Berlin. Mother – my step-mother – wanted so much to go back to Germany, but Karen insisted on staying in England. I

115

wanted her to come. There were jobs open for both of us. Secretarial. But she said there was still so much to learn in England. Wanted to spend a year playing at being an *au pair* girl. Those were her words. Father and Mother couldn't do much about it. She'd retained her German nationality. She was an alien. I tried to talk her out of it because I was worried. Things Karen had said.'

'Things? What sorts of things?'

'Oh. People she had met. In those last six months in England she had become... Oh, I don't know. Anti. Always criticising.'

'She was only twenty-three.'

'I'm only twenty-five.'

'Sorry.'

'Karen had changed. Mixing with odd people. I can't explain. We didn't meet any of them. She told me things.'

'You went back to Germany. She stayed in England and disappeared.'

Petronella bit her lip, hard. 'Yes. Last year. Mother had a breakdown. Then three weeks ago I had a letter from her. From Karen.'

'You've got it?'

'No, I burned it. It didn't really tell me anything. Except that she was alive and frightened.'

'Why burn it?'

'I was so … I don't know. I had to destroy it. Then I decided to come over and try to find her. The postmark was Bellinzona. I had some holiday due and I was already booked to go to London – for my Father. I was going to plan my search from there. Then the news came – while I was in London.'

'So you flew straight out.'

She nodded again.

'To do what?'

'I don't know. But I do know she was killed. Karen was killed. Murdered. It wasn't an accident.'

'And what about Penton?' Feeling very pleased about the way in which he slipped the question in, all unexpected. Petronella looked at him as though he was speaking Annamese.

'Penton?'

'Penton. William Francis Penton, Member of Parliament. And don't say you've never heard of him because you were talking to him under a willow outside this hotel last night. I saw you.'

Recognition. 'I thought I knew his face. Pompous little man. Made a pass at me.' She grinned for the first time since Boysie had found her. 'Come to that, so did you.'

It looked genuine enough. Boysie decided to give her the benefit of the doubt.

'And these?' He jingled the medallions together.

'The Hippogriffins.'

'Hippo…?'

'Griffins.'

'That's what I thought you said.' Boysie was curiously shocked.

'Isn't it a gear name? Daddy saw them in the Burlington Arcade before we left London.' She went solemn again. 'He bought them for us. For Karen and me.'

She was getting tearful again.

'So that's what a Hippogriffin looks like. I've always wondered.'

She swallowed. The tears remained un-spilled.

'I'm sorry. I should be hard shouldn't I? That's what we're supposed to be. The modern generation. Hard as ten-minute eggs. You don't know what a Hippogriffin is, do you?'

'It's an animal with a horse's body and an eagle's head.'

'Brilliant. The Hippogriffin was dreamed up by old Ariosto as a symbol of fantasy.'

'Of course,' said Boysie, brows wrinkled. Things were getting more and more compli-

118

cated. Kadjawaji, which meant Redland were nudging away somewhere in the background; the Wheater girl with her amber nine trouble – whatever that was – and the message for her Pa; Penton hanging around; Klara Thirel and her academy; Griffin getting awkward. He could manage without old Ariosto.

'Hippo Griffin,' said Boysie, making it apply to Griffin. Sounding very vulgar. He threw the medallion on to the bed. Petronella picked it up holding it in the palm of her hand, caressing it with her thumb.

'You feeling all right now?'

She wrinkled her nose and smiled. 'I must look terrible. Sorry I jumped to conclusions.'

'That's OK. Those friends of Karen's. And the letter.'

'Yes?'

'Tell me about them?'

'It's hard. There wasn't anything you could put your finger on. She just started changing. When we first got back to London she never stopped saying how wonderful everything was. Then there was this, sort of slow change. She wasn't happy any more. Went off by herself. Jeered at things. Talked about being progressive.'

'Political?'

Petronella looked as if she was trying to fight her way through a gale. 'Mnn, not really, yet I suppose there were political things. Yes, she was a member of CND. That's political, isn't it?'

'I should have thought so. And the letter?'

'What about it?'

'What was in it? What did she say?'

'It was like, as though she was drunk. Or drugged. She said she was sorry for any pain she caused. That she had gone away to help with something she believed in. To be alone with others who felt the same way. Then she found she had gone too far. It was a frightening letter. They were following her, she said.'

'Who were following her?'

'Just "they." No details. All jumbled.'

'Look, love.' Hesitant, trying to be mentally nimble. 'I think we may be on to something important. I want you to go to your room, lock the door and don't let anyone in until I get back. I won't be long. Will you do that?'

'I'm on this floor. Along the passage. 480. Yes.' She stood up and pushed a hand through her rusty hair. 'Can I keep this?' The medallion and chain still twined round her fingers.

'For the time being. May need it later.'
Boysie crossed to the door. She came to
him.

'You will help, Boysie, won't you? You'll
get the bastards who killed Karen?' Putting
a hand on his shoulder, pulling him towards
her. Her cheek was damp. 'Please help me.'
The words individually stressed coming
from the back of her throat. Her lips sticky
just below his ear. Boysie could not even
help himself. He did not stand a chance.

'Don't you worry. It'll be all right.' His
nervous system was declaring total war on
his basic instincts. In spite of the dwarf and
his lot, or Penton, Griffin, Mostyn, Klara,
Lynne Wheater or old uncle amber nine and
all, he would start things rolling because
here was a gorgeous girl whose figure made
you think of hay lofts on long Sunday
afternoons and whose legs went up and up
for ever.

'I'll wait in my room. Don't be long.' She
was out of the door, her make-up still
smudged where the tears had run.

'Oh gawd,' thought Boysie. 'What have I
done to deserve this?'

The pay-phone was about five hundred
yards from the hotel, near the pier where the
steamers chugged out to slide across the lake

121

on tourist excursions. After some language difficulty Boysie got the Department of Justice. After even more language difficulty he got Gatti who was civil but firm. Of course they had made enquiries at *Il Portone*. No one there had ever heard of the girl Schport. Thank you and good morning, Mr Oakes.

He got through to the continental exchange and reversed the call to the Bayswater number. It took twenty minutes. Two cigarettes. The girl at the other end sounded clean and hygienic. Efficient, Marks and Spencer skirt and blouse with the grey forced out and the white forced in.

'It's Roger here. My uncle in?'

'Hallo.' Gushing. 'How are you? Hang on I'll see if he's around.' The girl knew her stuff. Boysie idly started to count. '21 ... 22 ... 23 ... 24.' Click. That would be the transfer from Bayswater to Mostyn's Whitehall Office.

'Hallo. Roger?'

'Uncle James?'

'Yes. How's the weather over there?'

'Fine Winds light and variable.' It was bloody silly, but that was his identification.

'Have a good trip?'

'Not too bad. Bumped into an old friend.

122

Little dark fellow. Can't remember his name, but you know him. Could have been quite a circus on the train.'

'Like that, eh?'

Boysie pictured him, sitting back at that big desk. The tape turned on at the same time as his sarcastic smile.

'Met someone else this morning. Don't think you know her. Girl called Lynne Wheater. Look here, I wonder if you could do me a favour? She wants someone to ring her father in Wimbledon. Colonel Wheater at Wimbledon...' For a horrible moment Boysie's mind went dead. Was it 32697 or 32679. He threw in his lot with the law of averages. 'At Wimbledon 32697. Says she's got that amber nine trouble again.'

'Oh yes. Lucky meeting her.'

'Will you do that for me, uncle?'

'Of course, old boy.'

'She's out here at a finishing school – *Il Portone*. I think that's the name, have to check it. Met her principal. Woman called Klara Thirel.'

'Cyril?'

'No. At least I don't think so. Only introduced to her. Think it was a TH. Might be good place for the girls. I'm getting an invitation to visit anyway, so I'll let you know.'

'Well don't commit me to anything. Fees at those places are damned high. No harm in looking. Don't handle the goods too much though, Roger.'

'As if I would.'

'What about our business associate?'

'We're planning a meeting very soon. There's been some fun and games down here by the way. Girl drowned. Her sister's staying at my hotel. Step-sister that is. Name of Whitching. Father's in the RAF. Wonder if you've ever come across him.'

'Name rings a bell. Not the Wing Commander Whitching attached to the education people in Berlin is he?'

'Could be.'

'Glad you're enjoying yourself. When do you plan to come back.'

'Don't know yet. I'll call you when I've fixed that other deal. When I've seen the man.'

'All right, old son. Nice to have heard from you. Nothing else is there?'

'Don't think so. See you.'

'Look after yourself.'

The ambulance passed him – peep-parping and winking its light – heading in the direction of the hotel, just after he left the phone booth. He could see a large knot of people, signifying an accident, right outside the hotel. The road was blocked. By the time Boysie arrived and pushed his way through the crowd they were just loading the stretcher into the ambulance. The thing on the stretcher was covered with a white sheet through which large patches of bright red had begun to seep. There was blood smeared across the road, close by the pavement. A lot of blood. Boysie looked away, rapidly. He felt a little dizzy, his guts doing a dozen old-fashioned waltz steps. There was no sign of the vehicles involved.

Fighting his way to the main doors, Boysie found himself face to face with a worried-looking St Peter.

'What on earth's happened?'

'Oh, terrible Mr Oakes. A guest. Terrible.'

'What?'

'An accident. A guest has fallen from his balcony. On the top floor. The sixth floor. An old and valued guest.'

'Lord.'

'No, not a Lord. Worse Mr Oakes. A statesman. A countryman of yours. Mr Penton. Mr William Penton. Killed. Horrible.'

Safely back in his room, Boysie asked for the *Muralo*. Then Mr Goldblat. He was not in his room so they had to page him. At last Griffin's voice came on the line.

''Ullo.'

'Hallo, it's me.'

'Hallo then, got over your tantrums?'

'I was just calling to thank you.'

'Thank me? What the 'ell for?'

'Doing as I asked. For getting it over so quickly.'

'What the bloody 'ell you rabbitin' on about?'

'The bit of business we had. Thank you for doing it so neatly.'

'Doing it? Haven't done a bleedin' thing.'

'Well someone has.' Boysie thrown by the blood downstairs, felt light-headed. There was a pause. Like after you throw a grenade.

'The bleedin' nerve. You'd better get down 'ere and quick, mate. If you bin gettin' someone to undercut me I'll want to know why. Cor damn me. I'll be waitin' for yer. In the bar.' The line dropped dead, and Boysie clung to the table. He wanted to cry.

'Hippo-blasted-Griffin.' He said loudly. As though in answer there was a discreet knocking at the door.

The caller was a small flunkey bearing a salver upon which rested two white envelopes.

'Herr Oakes. Messages for you.' He grinned inanely. Boysie fumbled for the odd franc.

The first envelope was typewritten – as was the letter it contained:

Dear Mr Oakes,

It was pleasant to have met you this morning. I have been talking to Lynne and she feels a great deal happier about staying with us here at the school.

I have told her that you might be coming to visit us and have a look at our methods. She seemed happy at the prospect. I wonder if you would care to dine with me in my private apartment tonight at about seven-thirty. If you are free, just come along. It will be quite informal.

Yours in anticipation,
Klara Thirel.

The signature was bold, slightly mannish, undecorated. The notepaper bore the address, *Il Portone, Brissago, Lago Maggiore, Ticino, Switzerland,* in a blue 18 point Bembo Italic.

'Come into me parlour,' said Boysie quietly, ruminating on the possibilities of an evening with Klara. He looked at the other envelope. It was marked *By Hand* with his name written in a calligraphic snarl. The note had all the urgent dash of melodrama.

Please – I must see you. Can you be at the Madonna del Sasso at four? I will wait for an hour. Very important. Please – Lynne Wheater.

'It's a circus,' murmured Boysie. 'A three-ringed spangled circus.' Petronella upstairs; the comfortable Klara making spiderine noises from her lakeside lair, and now Lynne. 'The clowns or the acrobats. You pays your money.' He picked up the telephone. Downstairs St Peter was quick on the switchboard.

'What's the *Madonna del Sasso?*' asked Boysie.

'Ah,' said St Peter, clearing his throat for the guide-book bit. '*The Madonna del Sasso* is our sixteenth century sanctuary and place of pilgrimage erected on a crag behind and above the town. It is there in 1480 that the Madonna appeared to Brother Bartolomeo de'Ivrea...'

'Yes. But how do I get there?' The spiritual life of Brother Bartolomeo held no appeal for Boysie.

128

'There are two ways – up or down. By funicular from the Via Ramogna, near the station. Or along the Via Sasso and from there up the Via Dolorosa – it is a steep winding cobbled pathway marked by the Stations of the Cross. A favourite expedition is to go up by funicular and down by the path. It is very beautiful, Mr Oakes. The trees. The mountain greenery.'

'I'm sure.' Boysie asked to put through to 480. Petronella seemed content to wait in her room for another half-an-hour. There was the promise of luncheon at the end of her vigil. Boysie did not mention Penton.

Griffin was sitting at one of the little tables cluttering the main bar of the *Muralo*. He looked dejected and about to blast-off into tipsiness.

'Hallo. Shall we move on to the terrace?'

Griffin looked up. Reproachful. 'What you bloody playin' at then?'

'I'm not playing at anything. And keep your voice down.' Boysie propelled Griffin out on to the almost unoccupied terrace, and ordered a couple of *Campari* sodas. Griffin not speaking, looking sullenly at Boysie until the waiter had gone.

'Someone's done 'im then. Someone's done my bloke.'

'Either than or a fortuitous accident.'

'Fortuitous.' Griffin, pursing his lips and slewing them to the right as though tasting the word. 'Fortuitous. Such as?'

'Such as falling off a balcony.'

'Ah.' Griffin took a swig at his drink. 'Careless. Very careless and shoddy work. Who done it?'

'How the hell do I know. It could have been an accident. I've said.'

'Sound likely?'

'No, of course it doesn't.'

'Well then.'

'Well what?'

'Well then I'd like...'

'To know who done – did – it.'

'Yes.'

'So would I.'

'You sure you don't?'

'Of course I'm sure.'

'I mean it would be unethical and I'd 'ave to take steps. If you'd employed anyone else after contracting me.'

'Litigation already,' sighed Boysie.

'Don't try and come the big words with me, Mr Oakes. I'm a plain bloke.'

'All right. All right. No I did not hire anyone else. Don't be so touchy. I wouldn't bring you all the way out here and then use some local talent. People like you don't grow on trees. I mean one doesn't find you lot hanging around…'

'I'm not in favour of it meself.'

'No. You know what I mean.'

'Yea. But I still wants me money.'

'You'll get it.'

'Wouldn't mind findin' out who did it either.'

'I'm staying on to make a few enquiries.'

'Bit o' sleuthin' eh? You got a bird down here?'

'Certainly not. Well not exactly.'

'Ah. It'll be interesting to see what yer goin' to dig up. I wants me poppy and I'll be 'ere when you find out who took over the job. Got any ideas?'

'A couple. I've got a meeting this afternoon, and I'm going out to a finishing school tonight.'

'Could run one o' them meself. Finishin' school.' Griffin had turned jokey. 'Birds' finishin' school?' With interest.

'Out of your class, old Griffin.' Boysie all Mostynian. 'Mad discipline, health and all that. Probably dead dull. You know, folkweave nut cutlets and yoghurt injections.'

Boysie slipped away while Griffin was trying to work it out.

Back at the *Palmira* he despatched a cable to Mostyn at the Bayswater address. It read:

CUSTOMER SATISFIED STOP HOPE TO EXTEND BUSINESS STOP ROGER

Petronella was sitting patiently in her room when Boysie arrived. She looked happier, her face re-cosmeticised, her body partially covered by a striking little number in blue slubbed silk.

'Lunchies?' smiled Boysie.

'Lovely.' The lips looked comestible.

'Then a funicular ride.'

'Boysie!'

'Up the mountain to the *Madonna del Sasso*.'

'Oh. For a moment…'

'You thought that I was being vulgar. People always do.'

CHAPTER SEVEN

BLUE STEEL: LOCARNO

Boysie's telephone call, routed through the Bayswater house, disturbed Mostyn. The sub-text of the conversation was plain. Boysie's great clod-hopping boots had stirred the opposition. Things were happening down in Ticino. He listened to the tape just once, to make sure, and checked through the card index in his 'Most Personal' drawer. Kadjawaji was on the loose. That was obvious. Nasty. Mostyn picked up the yellow internal telephone.

'Number Two. Give me the DO.'

'Duty Officer.'

Mostyn had an accurate ear for voices. 'Number Two. That Martin?'

'Yes, sir.'

'Hole in one. Long time no see.'

'No, sir.' Martin was an old friend who had served much of his time with the Department as a stake-out man at London Airport.

'Old House-martin, eh?'

Martin allowed himself a thin smile, winking on and off as though controlled by a time-switch.

'Can I help you, sir. I've only got another five minutes on duty.'

A blizzard of silence. Then. 'How long have you been out of the field and on the DO's roster, Martikins?'

'A couple of months.'

'And how long with the Department?'

'Nearly five years.'

'Then you should know by now, friend, that the Department owns you. It has bought you body and soul – wretched and unworthy though you may well be.'

'Yes, sir,' a resigned note. Martin should have known better than to mention the imminent end of his tour of duty.

'I seem to remember,' Mostyn's voice had a feigned lilt of nostalgia, 'that you and I, old Martin, once had dealings with jolly old "L".'

Martin's right kneecap disintegrated in a mushroom of pain. This was the man's built-in warning system – a kneecap which hurt blindly at the approach of danger. Unerring as an aneroid barometer. He certainly remembered the dealings with 'L'.

'Yes,' Martin, unimpressed.

'Looks as though you're going to be concerned with him again, brother Martin.'

No reply.

'Action then, Martin.'

'Tape running, sir.' Clear and professionally efficient now.

'Right. Operational Area, Yodelcountry. Complete checkout of girl's finishing school called *Il Portone* near Locarno on Lake Maggiore. Secondary, check out Principal of school. Name, Klara Thirel, repeat K-L-A-R-A-T-H-I-R-E-L. No details. Third, check out with East Berlin Cell Four. Trace movements Indian midget known as Kadjawaji. Spell K-A-D-J-A-W-A-J-I. Active Berlin six to seven years ago and heavily involved Redland. Reported identified Yodelcountry yesterday. Four. Check out telephone number Wimbledon 32697 and occupant called Wheater. Final. Check all sections knowledge of code or operation or anything under Amber Nine. Repeat. Colour Amber. Figure niner. Fullest security screen all. Report direct to Number Two.'

'OK action, sir. Close?'

'Yes. Close.' Then the wolf in Mostyn's voice. 'Come up and see me, old Martin. That would be nice. For old times sake.

135

Come up before you go off duty, eh?'

'Very good, sir.' Unhappy.

Mostyn jabbed at the receiver rests, got through to the exchange switchboard and asked for the Chief Supervisor.

'Bill?' Silky. On the edge of a proposition. 'Number Two. Wanted to talk about Martin, good type on your Duty Officer's roster – used to be on stake-out at London Central. Couldn't lend him to me could you? Just for a few days. Attached to me direct.' The voice nattered quietly in the earpiece. Bill trying to ingratiate himself. Mostyn smiled. 'Bless you, Billy boy. As from the end of his DO period tonight. That is as from now.' Mostyn felt pleased. He had taken action, anticipating the further trouble which he instinctively knew was building up over the horizon and around Boysie.

'Kadjawaji left Berlin three days ago. Nothing yet on this Klara woman, *Il Portone*, or the Wheater person.' Mostyn shuffled the small sheaf of information flimsies. Martin sat glum on the opposite side of the desk. They had been together for an hour. Movements had sent up a passport, money and ticket for the night flight to Zürich – Martin was suddenly transformed into a travelling man. Information came on the line for Mostyn. He wrote, unseen nails creating creases in his brow as the invisible operator talked into his ear.

'Well, that's it. There seems to be a blanket of stealth surrounding *Il Portone* and this Klara Thirel. Military Intelligence got quite shirty. Something odd there. They say we have to get special clearance from Supreme Control. Amber Nine turned out to be one of the continental air roads and the cable address of some electrical engineers in Surbiton. They're sending details. Nothing on Wheater.' The telephone rang out again. Mostyn scribbled.

'"L"'s been busy bless him. Evening papers will have it I expect. Penton's out of the running. High dive off a hotel balcony. Quirky way of completing the old life cycle. But "L" is following his nose – thinks he's on to something and you know where that can land us.' Worry scratched into Mostyn's voice. Then authority again. 'You will retrieve, old Martin. Like a good gun doggie. Bring 'im back alive if you can. Oaksie has his uses.'

Martin sighed. Temperamentally he was a man good for sitting, watching and making accurate reports. Not a man of action.

137

Briefly he contemplated telling Mostyn but the direct line intercom, which ran between the Chief's office and Mostyn's desk, gave its ridiculous little toot.

'You alone, Number two?' The Old Man sounded too sober for comfort.

'No, Chief. Will be in a minute though.'

'Who's with you?'

'Martin. Sending him out to retrieve and give support on the "L" assignment.'

'Good. Just heard that Penton's dead. Fall from an 'otel window in Switzerland, poor chap. Just had one of me contacts in the Street on to me.'

'Haven't had time to report to you yet.' Mostyn quickly countered the implied criticism.

'No. Too busy askin' questions about Wheater and a telephone number in Wimbledon.'

'You what?'

'And a woman called Thirel.'

'Yes.'

'And a high-bloody-class finishing school called *Il Portone*.'

'Nothing else?'

'That's a blasted 'nough. But throw in Amber Nine – whatever that is. Trouble with this bloody job is that all our fornicating departments, inter-bleedin' service sections, the lot, are so blasted secret that they never let their own left hands know what the right hands are doin'. No bloody co-ordination or co-operation.'

'What seems to be the matter, Chief?'

'We mustn't meddle with the missin' *au pair* girl's thing for a start.'

'Who says?'

'SB've just been on. Shouldn't 'ave given us the info in the first place. They've had a rocket from Supreme Control – you know what those fellas are like.'

'Ancient Order of Buffaloes.'

'Better get up here, Number Two. What with your Wheater and such you've stirred up something. Inadvertently you've been treadin' on sacred ground. Very sacred. Top sacred as you might say.'

'Oh. Yes, Chief. Right away. I'll be up right away.'

Mostyn was rattled. Martin looked at the Second-in-Command with a new sense of understanding.

The luncheon had been pleasant, under a cool blue restaurant awning which stretched the length of the *Palmira's* façade. Chilled Melon and *Caneton Braise* – the white waiter, shoulders glistening with gold, carving the duck with the concentration of a surgeon performing a partial gastrectomy. The simile was accurate. He was assisted by a couple of junior waiters and watched by three trainees. Somewhere in the background, the head waiter stood poised, breath held and eyes fixed on the sliding-blade of the carving knife.

'You could sell tickets,' said Boysie. Petronella laughed. The head waiter looked scandalised.

They finished with *Himbeere Kaltschale* – because Boysie liked the name (it turned out to be raspberry purée) – and lingered over the coffee. For the first time that day Boysie's mind had a chance to reflect on the facts. He did not like what he found. The promise to help Petronella, and his readiness to meet Lynne were obviously dragging him deeper into something which he preferred to leave alone. Boysie began to sense the first returning quivers of anxiety. By the time they set out for the funicular ride to the *Madonna del Sasso* the quivers had turned into judders.

The *Drahtseilbahn* – funicular – which runs between Locarno and the *Madonna del Sasso* climbs for nearly a thousand yards, at a terrifying angle up the mountainside. At the rear of the car, crushed against the window between Petronella and a voluble lady in black, Boysie became fascinated by the stranded steel cable paying out behind them. Not for him the grey rock fascia or the network of fern and fir. To Boysie, disaster was in the air. Already he could see the cable giving way – a vivid picture of the car splintering down the long single rail with sparks showering: then the hideous crunch as they smashed through the terminus below. The car, designed to hold around eighty people, seemed oversubscribed – mostly with large perspiring pilgrims of Italian origin chanting a hymn in raucous semi-unison. Boysie only hoped it was directed at some saint whose patronage covered funiculars and similar appliances. There was a lurch (a dramatic change in the level of Boysie's stomach contents) and they arrived at the upper terminus.

The great baroque sanctuary of the *Madonna del Sasso* is approached, from the funicular, through a broad cloister circling the building. The west end rises in pink rococo curves, surmounted by a garish mural depicting Brother Bartolomeo having his vision. When Boysie and Petronella arrived, only a handful of people wandered about the gravelled square in front of the main doors. In the luke-warm bath of spring sunshine, perched high above the toy houses – the lake like a painted glass ornament – they seemed to be suspended in a sort of fairy-tale atmosphere. Boysie took particular notice of the sign pointing back through the cloister to the mountain path – the *Via Dolorosa* which they planned to use for the descent once Boysie had talked to Lynne. But there was no sign of the nervous Miss Wheater outside the church.

Inside, the cool ecclesiastical draught hit them – the familiar church chill mingled with a sweet smell of snuffed candle smoke and incense. Boysie looked round with wonder. This was his country. The heavy grey walls were covered with small bright paintings – some expertly executed, some crude, fascinating as wild brush strokes of children. All depicted the near-disaster, accident, or calamity from which their donor had been saved. A cart crashed over the edge of a precipice; a party of climbers swooped to their deaths leaving one lone figure clinging to a rock; a parachutist floated clear of a burning aircraft (undoubtedly aerodynamically unsound in the first place); a car hung half-way over a cliff. This Boysie could understand. People thanking an unknown deity for salvation from the kind of terrors which so often beset him. He could have searched the museums and art galleries of the world, but nowhere could he have found such a collection of paintings which summed up the night horrors and nervous fantasies which patinated his system.

'It's not exactly the Louvre, is it?' said Petronella stuffily.

'No, but there's more anxiety to the square inch here than in the London Clinic.'

Boysie was oblivious to everything but the pictures. He meandered around the build-ing, pausing, immersed in each group of canvasses. Completing the circuit back to the west door he realised he had lost Petron-ella *en route*. He swung round, taking in the whole religious scene. Not a sign of the neat blue figure. Nor of Lynne. The hands of his watch showed 4.15. For a second time, Boysie's eyes raked slowly around the church. Petronella must have gone outside.

As he stepped into the square he had to blink, readjusting to the brightness. Little orange and mauve dots floated in the foreground of his vision. Still no Petronella. No Lynne. Walking over to the sign which indicated the path to the *Via Dolorosa* he aimlessly followed it in the hope that Petronella had wandered on ahead of him. At the end of the cloister a set of narrow stone stairs led to a cobbled pathway sloping to the first zig-zag footpath which runs sheer down to the town. Boysie decided to go on to the next hairpin turn. If Petronella was not on the path he would go back. The cobbles were rough, hard under his sandals, with tricky smooth areas which made walking a full-time occupation. As he neared the turn, Boysie could make out the gable-shaped housing that enclosed the Fourteenth Station of the Cross. Thirteen angled bends, similar to this, lay below. As he drew abreast of the Station – stonework chipped and paint peeling – Boysie heard the rattle of a small dislodged pebble behind him. He turned. The man was coming down fast, eyes fixed on Boysie. Petronella was not round the corner. Only the other man. Boysie spun, his back against the Station. They were placed on either side of him, big blond boys dressed identically in suits of blue denim, their hair bleached golden by the sun. Each carried a smooth heavy walking stick. Boysie froze, like a child playing 'statues', taking in the denim suits, bronzed faces – one with a hawk nose, the other with a nasty white scar on his left cheek which must have made him brutally interesting to women. Someone laughed. Then the men – as if to order and in slow motion – brought their walking sticks across their bodies, grasping them with both hands high up. Hands twisting in unison. Two clicks and a shshshshnick. The sticks were drawn away, and Boysie was left looking into the glinting blue steel of a pair of rapiers.

The hook-nosed man had been standing a shade closer to Boysie than Scarface. As he operated his swordstick the heavy wooden scabbard slid from his fingers and bounced between Boysie and his partner. Boysie reacted with that natural panic-speed of a man desperate to save his skin. He leaped forward, fingers grasping at the stick, and swung upwards in a mighty cloud. There was a yell as the stick made contact with beak-nose's wrist. The rapier dropped and the man twirled obscuring his partner's vision for a vital second. Boysie, now engaged and having drawn blood, lashed out again, this time catching the whirling disarmed swordsman horribly behind the right ear. He fell, bumping against the one with the scar, and rolling dangerously near the edge of the path.

Boysie dived again. This time for the rapier. His hands curled round the hilt, recovering just in time to face the first lunging attack from his right. He made a lucky, fumbling semi-circular parry. There was a tingling clash of steel. By the jolt on his wrist, Boysie knew he was up against a professional. Scarface tried to *riposte,* the point spearing through Boysie's defence. But Boysie managed an *envelopment,* circling his opponent's blade to the right, backing away on the defence. He was surprised how it all came back so quickly. He could have been in the gymnasium with the high windows at Special Security's training centre fast among the sheep and skylarks of Hampshire.

Scarface came in again, point circling then beating at Boysie's blade. *Attack! Parry! Riposte!* Like a lesson. But Boysie was gradually being forced back to the bank. Vainly he tried to attack, lunging in high. Scarface carried out a neat *croise* and moved in close. The two blades slithered hard together and both men were locked tightly, wrist against wrist, *corps-à-corps.* Boysie again cursed the long winter. His muscular reserve was not what it should have been. Allowing his arm to give way slightly – putting Scarface off-balance – he pressed hard to the side and back. They disengaged. Scarface stumbled to the right. A moment of truth. Boysie did the one thing possible. He wheeled round and ran down the path. A shout from behind. He could hear Scarface thudding after him. Skidding and slipping, Boysie took the corner by the Thirteenth Station and careered on over the hazardous cobbles. Twelfth. Eleventh, Tenth. Scarface was gaining. At the ninth corner the gradient flattened a little – a tall fir surrounded by a spur of earth, Scarface was nearly on him. Breathless, Boysie turned, his back against the tree. Scarface slowed, slipped into the *en garde* position and came on with a series of lunges to the throat. Once more, steel flickered against steel. Boysie beat the blade away. Then, suddenly the fang of blue metal was coming fast for his stomach. Boysie parried, but the blade, knocked downwards, came on. It was like a burn high on the inside of his right thigh and there was a small thump as the point slid into the tree trunk, accurate between his legs. Boysie lunged and saw his blade make contact with Scarface's shoulder. The denim ripped and a blotch of blood spread like red ink on blue blotting paper. Scarface gave a small moan, let go of his rapier and staggered backwards, leaving the impaled weapon waving obscenely like a broken metronome. Boysie moved in to consolidate his victory with a variation of the *Chavante* arm lock – cupping the left hand under the opponent's right elbow pushing upwards, while at the same time the right hand levers down on his right wrist. The result, in the case of Scarface, was a broken arm and unconsciousness.

Boysie fell back against the tree. The aftermath of fear. His thigh stinging and a fair straggle of blood showing on his trousers. He limped on down the path to the Via Sasso. In the sunlight a Grecian white Victor Estate car stood proud and opulent. Slight blurring of Boysie's sight. Beside the estate car were two visions – dream legs ending in leather short-shorts, grey shirts, heads crowned with golden haloes. They were moving towards him. The ground swayed. Behind them, a shorter neat figure. Boysie could not feel his legs. It was as though he was floating toward the car. Chrome-edged windows. The feel of metal on his shoulder.

'Why, it's Mr Oakes. Quick, girls. Help him. He's ill. Or had an accident.' As though through water, Boysie could see the face of Klara Thirel. 'Into the car with him. Quickly, idiot child. Quickly.' Soft hands and arms round his legs and shoulders. Then a dizzy half-knowing.

'Fools,' said Klara Thirel. 'Come, Ingrid. Move.' Her hand caught the blonde a swipe across her leather-clad backside. Ingrid shrugged and slid into the driving seat. 'You first, Angela.' Klara almost pushing the other girl into the back of the car. 'Quickly, quickly, quickly.' Angela got in, hunched up near Boysie who was sprawled over the seat. Last, Klara pushed herself in on the other side of Boysie.

'Back to the school. As fast as you have been taught, Ingrid, or the whips will be out tonight,' said Klara Thirel, a pleased grin spreading over her face. The car moved off towards the lakeside road which leads to Ascona and Brissago.

CHAPTER EIGHT

WHITE VIRGINS: BRISSAGO

Martin was sipping his coffee in the Departure Lounge of No 2 Europa building in London Airport, remembering the times he had loitered, with intent to observe, around the halls, escalators and bars of the gehenna which shovels souls in and out of the metropolis. He had enjoyed that time as stake-out man at London Central: lurking, watching (and watching for) people. Over five years he had learned everything there was to know about each square inch of steel and glass, each chip and stain in the fabric of the place. Now, on the other side of the fence, he had two hours to wait. By this time young Duncan, or one of the other boys, would have reported the fact that he was in transit. Two hours to wait before flashing off into the sky: thundering into the night. That expression made Martin feel a bit more glamorous – a real live Eastmancolor-type spy. Martin, the agent, thundering off into the night on a mission. It had a good ring to it, even though in his heart of hearts he knew that a vile attack of wind, caused by airline food, was all the thundering into the night would ever do.

Mostyn had whipped him out to the airport in double-quick time. The Second-in-Command had been up in the chief's office for about twenty minutes, returning with a face the colour of a ripe Victoria plum, hands dancing like nervous puppets.

'Some,' Mostyn had said, 'should be doctored. Hands off the *au pair* scandal, that's the word.'

'Whose?'

'Whose what?'

'Word.'

'Director of Supreme Control. And we all know who he is – bloody little Jack-in-Office. Chief's given his oath that we haven't take any action. Denied we had anyone in the field in that area.'

'Had to really, didn't he? It being the Oakes boy.'

'Yees.' Mostyn drew the word out facing the fact reluctantly. 'The darlings are jumpy as rabbits in clover. One of the Departments has obviously got something big going on. Major operations. Churning it, Martin, old horse. Churning it with dear old Special Security left right out in the snow. Mustn't even whisper words like Wimbledon, *Il Portone,* Thirel, Wheater or Amber Nine. Mustn't whisper 'em let alone ask questions. Lord help us if Boysie's got himself tangled in anything.'

'Important I get him out quickly then. More important than ever.'

'You're joking of course. Even broken the rules and telephoned his hotel. He's out. With a Miss Whitching if you please. Left a message telling him to phone his uncle as soon as...'

'He gets back...'

'Yes. As soon as he returns from his libidinous excursion.'

Martin did not know that once Mostyn had scooped him into the Zephyr outside HQ, the 2 I/C had made a record dash back to his office. Mostyn was equipped with too much of an enquiring mind to leave a shroud of grey mystery hanging over the clamp-down which had pressurised the Department of Special Security since Boysie's telephone call. Mostyn always preferred to be at least one jump ahead of everybody. On a blank sheet of paper he wrote a list of the offending names. He sat and looked at them.

for a long time, then picked up his red scrambler telephone.

'Give me Central Four.'

Central Four – Mostyn's opposite number in the Special Branch – came on the line.

'Hallo, James.' The voice could, at a nip, be taken for yet another Mostyn. 'Just been talking about you. To my boss.'

'Strange. Just been talking about *you*. To *my* boss.'

'Oh yes.' Central Four sounded disinterested, in a cat and mouse way.

'Yes.' Firm.

'Anything I can do for you, James?' Slinky.

'Seem to remember you owe me a couple of favours, old lad.'

'No can do James. Not if it's the *au pair* thing, no can do.'

Mostyn silently breathed a word not usually associated with Civil Service procedure. 'What about Colonel Wheater of Wimbledon?'

'The shutters are up, James. This is not – repeat not – any of Special Security's business. Now, please, keep out. It ain't your pigeon.'

Robin Villiers – a very high-ranking member of MI5 – pulled the same poker-faced stunt. So did Bonzo Innes at MI6.

Trying his last card Mostyn called the Personal Secretary to the Director of Supreme Control – a pasty young man with protruding teeth who fancied Mostyn's younger sister Geraldine. The PS to the DSC was very rude. Mostyn, furious and frustrated, decided to tell Geraldine that he knew, for a fact, the young puppy had been having it off with a WREN Third Officer. The fury and frustration turned to anxiety. He was fumbling in the dark and it was bloody black.

At London airport, the Public Address system came to life. 'Swissair regret that owing to a minor technical fault their Coronado flight SR 101 will leave approximately one hour later than its scheduled time.' Martin looked at his watch. Two and three-quarters hours to wait.

Twice Boysie managed to pull himself out of the dizzy daze in the car. Vaguely it occurred to him that the rapier points had been drugged. He had not lost enough blood to make him this woozy. Each time he looked up his watery vision took in a blue of lakeside road moving fast. There was a smell of crushed strawberries. Female breasts rubbed against his shoulders. Both shoulders. What kind of woman *was* this? Eventually because the sensation was so pleasant, Boysie gave up fighting and allowed a clerical grey mud to slush over the bulk of his brain. Now he was Hamlet having the final duel with Laertes. Christ, Kadjawaji was playing Claudius. No, was he hell: it was Mostyn, blacked-up, sitting there with the crown square on his head and that damn great sceptre, and Petronella as Queen Gertrude next to him. Rot Mostyn, he was after Petronella now.

Half of Boysie's numbed senses felt the car stop. Gertrude, or somebody, said, 'Let four captains bear Boysie, like a soldier to the stage.' He was being lifted. He forced the eyelid muscles to work. Grey shirts amiably filled with girl. Soft, tender faces looking down.

'My god that stuff's potent. He's only had a scratch, and look at him,' said Klara Thirel.

'A hit. A palpable hit,' drowsed Boysie as he sank into a great pile of swansdown.

It was a sensation he had never experienced before. Not the slow waking from a long sleep – that drag up the hill to consciousness – but a new, quick way of coming back to life. One minute he was away; the next, wide awake, alert, refreshed. The smell of crushed strawberries was still in the air and one of the grey-shirted blondes was bending over him.

'He's awake, Principal.'

Boysie sat up. He was lying on a bed, at the foot of which stood Klara Thirel. The room was cool: décor light grey; two tall windows open – heavy blue curtains swinging to the occasional stir of air – spring flowers on a table near the door; a couple of modern chairs; on the wall opposite the bed a Walter Keane lithograph – it looked like *La Scunizza* – a waif's saucer eyes engulfing Boysie from the frame. Somewhere, far away, Sammy Davis and Paula Wayne wanted to be with each other in stereo.

'Angela, tell the girls to turn that record player down. Now! Pronto!' said Klara rather bossily. Angela straightened up and walked, like a tall cat, to the door.

Boysie looked down the length of his body. The clothes were not his. A cream nylon shirt and tight denim trousers. He moved, realising that the comforting bump of the Sauer & Sohn was not there in his hip pocket. Boysie allowed his hands to slide over the shirt. The movements were vague, uneasy.

156

'Who...?' He started.

'Undressed you?' Klara smiled – a full, knowing, sophisticated smile. 'Please don't worry, Mr Oakes. We have several trained nurses here. It was all most respectable.'

'I should hope so. What is all this anyway?' He swung his legs off the bed. Checked himself, expecting to feel muzzy. He was quite steady.

Klara ignored the question. 'There are some sandals for you. On the floor. I only hope that they fit.'

'What the hell happened?' He could remember the duel. Since then, only a day-dream sequence. His thigh was throbbing.

'You looked as though you had been in some kind of an accident.' Her speech was precise, but without the clipped self-consciousness, or the studiously correct grammar which often distinguishes the well-educated Middle-European. 'We couldn't just leave you there. So, as we were hoping for your company tonight anyway, we thought it best to bring you straight along. Instead of taking you back to your hotel. Or the hospital. Are you feeling all right?'

'Fine,' said Boysie mistrusting every word. His hand strayed to his thigh. Under the denim he could feel a wound dressing of

157

some kind. Klara Thirel detected the questioning look.

'You have a rather nasty scratch there. It was not necessary to provide stitches. Angela put a dressing on it and gave you a shot of penicillin.'

'Did she now!' Boysie felt himself blushing. He slid his feet into the sandals. They were a size too large but he would manage.

'You really are all right now?'

'Like I said. Fine.' The next move was up to him. 'I suppose I'd better telephone the hotel. Messages and that kind of thing.'

'We've already taken care of that. They know where you are; any calls will be transferred here. You see, for a girls' finishing school we are really very efficient.'

'Yes, I thought you would be.' Then, craftily. 'How's Lynne?' She wouldn't be expecting that one so soon.

Klara Thirel smiled again. Not altogether friendly. Like a school Matron of your first day. Sadistic. 'She's been confined to the sick bay but you may see her before you go.'

Boysie tried to work out whether she meant that he might see her, or that he would be allowed to see her. He glanced at his watch. Seven thirty. He had been out for less time than he thought.

'Well, if you're ready I should imagine the girls will be waiting.'

'For what?'

'Dinner, Mr Oakes. You're dining with us.'

'Oh yes?'

'I know I asked you to eat with me privately, but I've had second thoughts. It seemed a pity to deny the girls a treat.'

'You sound like a cannibal chief.'

Klara went off into a gust of laughter. 'I see what you mean. The girls. A treat. Ah, *filet d'Oakes*.' She looked very attractive – in a mature sort of way. Kinky even, still in the black polished riding boots and breeches – though the shirt was now a crisp blue matching her eyes. Boysie was conscious of danger, yet, strangely he did not feel his usual stomach-cramping fear. Perhaps his normal confidence with women helped to alleviate the nerves and restore a balance. He took a pace towards Klara, automatically putting out a hand, fingers touching the woman's shoulder.

'Aw, call me Boysie,' he said almost bashfully. 'Everybody does.'

'Yes, I think I like that better.'

'Good.'

'Yes, *filet de Boysie* sounds more like a gourmet's dish.' A giggle turning into an

159

almost dirty guffaw. Klara steadied herself with a hand to Boysie's arm. They were close. There was tap on the door and handsome Angela high-stepped into the room. Klara turned slowly. A woman of some experience thought Boysie. Most girls would have pulled away quickly in a flurry. Angela looked hard at Boysie. Boysie's eyes dropped to his sandals. He was blushing involuntarily.

'Dinner is ready, Principal.'

'Good. Thank you, Angela. You may go down to the others now. I'll see the Seniors later.'

'Very good, Principal. I hope you're all right now, Mr Oakes.'

'Great.' Boysie still had his eyes fixed on his large shuffling sandals. Then he looked up straight at Angela. 'Just great.' Happy to see that there was a kind of admiration in the blonde's eyes.

It was like being in some fabulous harem. They passed out of the room into a wide hall. Facing them, large double doors, flanked by ceiling-high windows which looked out on to a broad snake of gravel. To the left an ornate lift cage into which Angela stepped. Boysie vaguely noticed that the blonde took the lift down. On the right, another set of double doors outside which stood a pair of delectable redheads – uniformed in thin white cotton shirts and the ubiquitous black leather short-shorts. As Klara and Boysie appeared, the girls opened the doors in unison. At the same time, the one on the left called out, 'School stand for Principal'.

'The Geschlechtlich twins,' whispered Klara.

'Ah,' said Boysie sagely.

'Nice girls. Daughters of the Baron Von Geschlechtlich. Good stock.'

From the other side of the doors came the scraping of chairs. There must have been a good 150 of them. A sea of white shirts which would have made a launderette manager drool, and leather short-shorts in abundance – one great beautiful mass of girls standing straight and sexy behind chairs along three refectory tables. At the top of the room the high tables flashed with studded silverwear. Everything – the girls, the room itself, cutlery, the serving tables down one wall, the three original Picassos – shouted wealth. As he followed Klara past the sinuous wall of backs, to the high table, Boysie could not help feeling that *Il Portone*

161

had a great deal to offer as far as this world's moth and rust corrupting goods were concerned.

From his vantage point between Klara and a bright brunette, Boysie saw nothing sinister in the pupils of *Il Portone*. He could have been in the dining hall of any expensive finishing school. Certainly the girls were stamped with a definite military obedience (the way they had stood as Klara entered, the manner in which they had reacted to her order, 'Sit, girls,' their almost over-correct postures, a rigidity of the back now they were seated). But they all looked pretty normal and well developed. The brunette on his right stretched out her hand and grinned an introduction.

'Mary Van Bracken. Boston, Mass.'

Boysie shook hands. The Van Bracken girl's grip decidedly firm. 'Boysie Oakes, London, Eng.,' said Boysie searching for something not too banal to counter the introduction. 'I didn't realise this was such a cosmopolitan place.' It was a lame gambit but the best he could muster.

'Oh gee, yes, we got them from all over,' said Mary Van B chirpily.

A shirt-covered breast grazed Boysie's right ear as a plate of smoked salmon was placed in front of him. He raised his eyes and did a square search of the tables. The resulting montage was itchily satisfying – long, beautiful fingers gently squeezing the juice from the lemon segments over pink slices; forks daintily conveying small rolled portions of fish from plates to ready, willing lips; teeth caressing, tongues savouring, Occasionally a pair of eyes – hazel drops, misty blue invitations, deep brown promises – flashed up at him, then away with disturbing eyelashes. Eating, as Boysie had noticed many times, could be very like a complicated love play.

The tinkle of wine in his glass caused him to turn his head. A *Saint-Croix-due-Monte*. He sipped. At a guess, '53. Doctor Thirel and her girls lived well. A razor blade of sharp ice scraped the short hairs on the back of Boysie's neck with the realisation that he was being lulled into a sense of well being. The incident that morning with Lynne Wheater and Doctor Thirel should have been enough warning about *Il Portone*. Since then had not a brace of swashbuckling thugs tried to skewer him against the mountainside? Lynne had not turned up. Petronella had disappeared. The *au pair* girls? Penton MP? Klara herself? A regiment of randy females. Good food and excellent wine. It was all far too easy. He bit into another slice of salmon. His perception seemed sharp, but there must still be some of the drug working in his system. Perhaps it had the same deceptive effect as alcohol which seems to stimulate yet really depresses. Boysie felt a sudden wave of sick terror. The feeling of ease had been accompanied by a slight drowsiness. He must fight. Watch it, Boysie. Case the joint. Look at the girls. Remember the *au pair* file – it was the only thing on which he could anchor.

Once more Boysie allowed his eyes to slide furtively around the tables. This time a thorough examination of the girls' faces. He got as far as an exquisite Chinese doll – half-way down the table to his left – when Klara spoke.

'You are interested in our school, Boysie. Mary here has been in residence for six months now. She would be a good person to talk with.' An admonishing note. For the first time, Boysie took in the other women who shared the top table. Mary Van Bracken was the only pupil. The rest were middle-aged or frankly elderly women – all dressed like Klara. The staff, he presumed – and a pretty rum lot they looked.

'I'm sorry,' said Boysie, forcing the charm. 'Not used to eating in the company of so many distractions.' He smiled at Mary Van Bracken, knowing it was coming out as a leer.

'What do you wish to know, Mr Oakes? I'm at your service.'

Boysie opened his mouth, then thought better of it. Finally, 'Well, your Principal tells me she uses – how did she put it – odd methods?'

The American girl laughed. 'True enough,' she shrugged. 'Why beat about the bush. Before we came here we were all, well, hard cases. You have to be from a certain strata of society to afford this place.' Mary pouted seriously. 'Lower down the scale every girl here would almost certainly have ended up in some juvenile delinquent home – reform school and all that. We've all been difficult teenagers and most of us fought like hell not to come here. But, you can see, it works.'

'What works?'

'Doctor Thirel's methods.'

'Tell me. What do you learn here?'

Mary looked at him. Boysie thought he detected a pinpoint of uncertainty in her eyes before she spoke. 'She is a very clever woman, Doctor Thirel. She has a knack at finding out where one's talents really lie.' She was getting excited now. Committed. 'Back home, at school in Boston, I was a nut at languages. Couldn't learn them. Had no idea how to approach a foreign tongue. Doctor Thirel explained that I was afraid of languages. I was setting up a mental block – because I wanted so much to be able to speak something other than Boston-flavoured English. I'm doing French, German, and Russian now. Loving it. Making progress.'

Boysie's security mechanism pricked up its antennae. 'Do many girls take German and Russian?'

'Why yes. Quite a few.' Mary looked blank. 'After all they're going to be the major commercial languages in Europe aren't they? I mean in a few years they're going to be almost obligatory for business.'

Boysie hoped he was not visibly shaken. 'And other talents? What other talents has the Doctor discovered?'

'Oh, the strangest things.' She was a prattling schoolgirl again. 'One of my room mates – my best friend actually – has developed a passion for contemporary European political history. Never had a thought in her head until she came to *Il Portone* – that is except for beat, boys and clothes. Amazing.'

'Amazing,' Boysie repeated, his head nodding like a plastic Alsatian in the back of a family car.

'Then there's Indra – the Pakistani girl over there.' She indicated with her eyes towards the remarkable features which could have been finely shaped from appetising coffee cream. 'She's doing twentieth-century political economy.'

Boysie took advantage of the following pause to look at another four faces. No recognition. 'I'd never have guessed any of these girls were hard cases,' he said.

'Some of them are not too easy to crack either,' Klara chimed in. 'Eh, Mary? Mary had a bad patch to start with.'

'Aw heck.' Sheepishly from Mary. 'But the Doctor's methods always win.'

'Tell me more.' Boysie found his interest growing. Girls from good backgrounds, with delinquent characters, being moulded, taught languages, political history and economics. A situation ideal for exploit-ation. A breeding ground for intriguers or intriguettes.

'Simple really. Military. If you're tough she can be tough. We have a system of punish-ment cells.' Mary giggled. 'You know you can be sent to jail for between seven and thirty days here?'

'Jail?' stated Boysie.

'Yep. And that can mean one of two things depending on your attitude. Either you can get it soft – just locked in a room with a lovely bed and TV...'

'Hu?'

Klara came back into the conversation. 'I can assure you that it is very humiliating to a girl who thinks she is being really clever – acting up to become some sort of martyr.' Turning her attention to the *Châteaubriant* which had just been served, oozing juices and running with *Maître d'hôtel* butter.

Boysie followed suit nodding. The nodding was getting habitual. 'I can see that.' Looking at Mary. 'And the other way?'

'The other way is really tough. Proper cells. And you're looked after by the Seniors. They can be bitch...' She braked her tongue before the word was wholly out. Klara Thirel's look was designed to maim at three paces. The Doctor smiled. 'Say it, Mary.' Gently. 'The Seniors can be bitches. That's what you were going to say. All women and girls can be bitches, Mary.'

'Seniors?' queried Boysie.

'This is only the Junior School. They wear

white shirts. We call them,' Klara paused, her face still in the set smile she had given Mary, 'we call them the Virgins. A vain hope I'm afraid, but I have a warped sense of humour.'

'The Seniors are the grey jobs then?'

'You could say that.' Cold.

Mary was anxious to reinstate herself. 'Most of the girls come here for a straight twelve or eighteen months. Some, who do well, are invited to stay on for another year.'

'You become a Senior by invitation only. That's important.' Klara was directing the conversation. 'We only have a dozen or so Seniors at any given time. They do advance studies and assist me. Like prefects.'

'And they can get rough?' Boysie was determined to hear it from Mary. The skin on his shoulders, and arms crawling with the apprehension that he was going to learn of something unpleasant under the calm surface of life at *Il Portone*.

'Oh, they can be rough. I know, Mr Oakes. The Principal told you, I was difficult when I arrived.'

'I'm sorry.'

'No need to be.' Bright. 'Did me the world of good.'

Boysie shrugged and continued to

demolish his *Châteaubriant* followed by a magnificent Fruit Zabaglione. Even the food at *Il Portone* was fashioned towards the sensual. He reluctantly dragged his mind back to the matters in hand. The Seniors were obviously a race apart. If this thesis was correct, the girls in grey shirts were graduates of Klara Thirel's academy: those invited to take special training for the cause. They lived in segregated quarters – somewhere below stairs, he imagined, having seen the fair Angela take the lift down from the ground floor.

The pish-pish of revolver shots fired near the building made Boysie's stomach turn turtle. Klara must have felt the jump. 'Don't worry. Only some of the Seniors,' she said sweetly. 'We keep a small firing range down on the lake-side. They like to go and try a bit of target practice about this time of day.'

A wiry rat-faced instructress sitting on Klara's left, joined in – a mannish, and very English, cut glass. 'Good for the gel's co-ordination. Hand, eye, brain. All that sort of thing. Like shootin' for the jolly old clay pipes at the fair.'

'The clay pipes,' said Boysie passively. Then, to himself, 'Three bullseyes and a couple of Virgins. A Teddy Bear and a plastic loofah for the girl with the 36B cup bust.' That just about clinched it. Shooting practice yet. Probably if he got a peek at the lawn they would be cavorting about doing Karate. This was it. A choice of actions. He could try and make his getaway, or cheekily stay and investigate the Seniors (Boysie's mind shuffled from the point at this last unfortunate turn of phrase). Natural inclination told him to take to the hills. Fascination bade him stay and meddle. It was not a question of bravery, or even the old loyalty, Queen-and-Country spiel. Rationalising, Boysie began to talk himself into the idea that if he stayed there was less likelihood of being injured, or even killed. Wild dashes for freedom had never been his strong point. After all, he might discover that he was over-dramatising the situation. *Il Portone* could – just possibly – turn out to be nothing more than a rather off-beat finishing school. Boysie curled his lip. He would stay. He was a match for any woman.

Opportunity for action came shortly after the meal finished. The girls had filed off to work once more.

'They have another hour of classes after dinner,' Klara explained before inviting him out on to the long, stone-flagged terrace which seemed to run round the entire area of the house. It was already getting dark and the last flush of sun had left the tinted garden stretching in a shallow slope down to the lake. From what he could see, Boysie deducted that the house itself lay about one hundred yards from the road, and about half that distance from the lake. To their right the village of Brissago was beginning to twinkle. Boysie leaned against the stone balustrade and blew a thin stream of smoke towards the dark lake. He could feel Klara's upper arm gently touching his – pins and needles at the first approach of sexual shock waves.

'What are those?' he pointed towards two dark humps which seemed to rise out of the water about a quarter of a mile from the shore.

'Those islands? The Isole di Brissago.' She sounded as though that was all there was to say about the matter.

'Inhabited?'

She laughed. 'Not by cannibals anyway. There's a boat house and largish villa. Tourist attractions now. Nice gardens though. The villa is permanently closed.'

Boysie was about to enquire further, but Klara quickly changed the subject. 'I wish you could see this view in sunlight. It's so beautiful. Therapeutic for some of my girls.'

'Well, maybe I can come back in daylight before I return home.'

A pause. 'Maybe.' She turned. A Senior – short with cropped hair and muscular outlines – had come on to the balcony.

'Principal?' Agitated. 'A word, please.'

'Excuse me.' Klara allowed her hand to rest momentarily on Boysie's arm as she moved over to the girl. There was a low rapid conversation with Boysie straining his hearing to full volume.

'Would you wait here for a minute, Boysie?' Klara returned, the hand again resting on his arm. The promise of something more if he stayed put. 'There is a matter which needs urgent attention. Please don't stray from the terrace. We have guards. You know. The girls. There are strict rules – and dogs, fierce dogs, I would hate you to get mistaken for a prowler or a Peeping Tom.'

'Never peeped in my life,' said Boysie, taking another drag on his cigarette and trying to look like Brando when the chips are down.

The Senior followed Klara Thirel into the villa. Boysie waited a full two minutes before slipping back into the dining hall. He crossed to the doors, gently trying the handles. They opened silently. Cautiously he edged out into the hall. Once more at the crossroads. The way to both the front entrance and the lift was clear. Boysie closed his eyes and took a deep breath, on the edge of indecision. Fascination again won through. Six paces, clumsy because of the oversize sandals, took him to the lift. The outer gates slid back and he instinctively pressed the lowest in the row of operating buttons. The lift dropped and he was descending through a smooth steel shaft. Fifteen seconds and the cage reached bottom. Boysie found himself in a high-roofed hall. The walls were white and bare, lit by two long strip-lights running the length of the ceiling. A thick grey carpet covered the floor. Opposite the lift gates an archway led into a long corridor which sloped downwards. Removing the hampering sandals, Boysie went through the arch and headed down the passage. It was about six feet wide, lit – like the hallway – by strip-lights, and covered with the same grey carpet. There was no sound except for the whisper of air conditioning, coming through gratings set flush against the roof at intervals of seven or eight yards. The temperature was pleasant and, even though he was obviously moving deeper and deeper underground – and, judging by the direction, underlake – Boysie could detect no dampness.

Suddenly, ahead and to the left, a voice, feminine and strident, yapped into the silence. 'Second position. Hup. Begin.' Followed by a deep rhythmic thudding. Boysie flattened against the wall, his heart beating to the drumming noise. Nothing happened. He moved on. The thudding got louder until he realised it was coming from behind a pair of heavy wooden swing doors – set into the wall on his left, each with a large upper window panel. Boysie, still taut against the wall, crept up to the doors and slowly pushed one eye into a peering position round the edge of the nearest panel. Boysie blinked. He was looking straight into a vast gymnasium in the centre of which about thirty girls – led by one of the strange lady teachers – were doing warming up exercise. Boysie felt the perspiration begin to mount the back of his neck. Girls were dressed only in tight white briefs and brassieres. Bodies rippling as they went through an intricate routine of lateral bending, arm circling and the dreaded partial sit-ups. It was a sight for sore eyes let alone optics that were blessed, like Boysie's, with twenty-twenty vision. 'On your backs, Hrrp!' Shrieked the muscular madam. Boysie's reflexes made him catch his breath. Thirty female bodies (in the pink of condition) were prostrate. 'On your stomachs. Rrroll!' Boysie's eyes glazed over. 'Legs Apart.' Boysie swallowed. 'Chest and leg raising. Begin!' Boysie smiled happily, propped on shoulder against the wall and felt for his cigarettes. Then he remembered where he was. Reluctantly he dropped to his knees and crawled under the panels of glass, well out of sight.

About one hundred yards further on a large notice warned 'Junior Girls Not Permitted Beyond This Point'. The passage flattened and turned sharply to the right. As he rounded the bend Boysie could see another archway which marked the end of the tunnel about fifty yards ahead. The thudding, from the gym, was still just audible, but now it was joined by other noises, floating into the passage from beyond the archway. A shout. A girl's voice raised in banter. Joan Baez asking what have they done to the rain?

The passage led into a hallway, similar to

the one by the left shaft. But here other corridors branched off to left and right. A third seemed to be a short continuation of the one through which he had just walked. The Joan Baez record thrummed out from the passage to his left. Boysie moved along the hall until he could look down this corridor at an angle. It was like a passage in an office block, with doors set at regular intervals. The first door, about four feet from the hallway, was wide open. Lying on a bed, very much in full view and reading *Homes and Gardens,* was the lithe Angela. She had discarded the short-shorts and her shirt was unbuttoned revealing a neat grey brassiere and easily dispensable bikini pants. Another girl sat with her back to the door. The Joan Baez came to an end.

'Want the flip side?' The girl in the chair spoke, husky with a slight Italian accent. Further down the passage, someone began to sing.

'Why bother,' said Angela. Shouting, 'The singing blackbird's off again.'

From three doors down a scrumptious girl, the colour of oiled ebony, stepped into the passage trilling. She was quite naked. Boysie leaned back out of sight – quivering. The coloured girl stopped in mid-bar (she

177

was singing 'I believe in you') long enough to suggest that the fair Angela was a colourless sex-fiend. Boysie felt oddly shocked. The 'I believe in you' songstress was muted by the bang of her door closing. Boysie peeped out again. Angela was laughing. The *Homes and Gardens* dropped to the floor and for a moment Boysie thought the girl was going to look straight at him. He pressed himself against the wall wishing he was a chameleon. Silence.

'It's tomorrow night then,' said the other girl.

'So they say. Klara promised to let me look at the operations room. There's one absolutely gorgeous man up there. The other two are a million years old, but this one – Russell – is super.'

'I should've thought you'd had your fill of supermen today after dealing with that Oakes person.'

'Instant cat,' thought Boysie. 'I wish I were a sadist.'

'Super-duper-duper-men,' mused Angela. The phrase seemed vaguely reminiscent. Angela continued. 'I would tell you things about him that would wrinkle your kinky boots, darling.'

'Hu!' Scorn.

'Anyway, you'll be seeing him yourself before long. Klara's bound to dump him down here with those two bright bitches.'

'And there's one of those I'd like to get my soft perspiration-free hands on. That Lynne vixen tried to bite my thumb off when we put her in.'

Boysie turned down the corners of his mouth, frowned and nodded. So they had Lynne and Petronella here. The cells? He shuffled back along the wall and crossed the hall out of the line of vision from Angela's open door. There was no sign of life in the continuance of the main passage, which went on for about twenty yards, ending in a massive steel door. Boysie walked back and tried the corridor to the right. This was also a short passage, but with two doors, ten paces apart, in the left-hand wall. Each was fitted with a large mortice lock – the keys hanging on small hooks to the left of the doors. At eye-level, pear-shaped slices of flat metal covered peep-holes. Boysie stopped at the first door, raised the cover and pressed his eye to the aperture. A bare cell, windowless and white – the light coming from some source high in the ceiling. Against the far wall was an iron bedstead. A girl lay face downwards. She wore tight faded jeans, naked from the waist up. Boysie's face crumpled. The girl's back was criss-crossed, like some monstrous railway layout, with angry red welts, the spaces between freckled with blood. She had been beaten – almost certainly with a thonged whip. From the peep-hole the young back looked like an abstract in violence. Boysie breathed a soft, unpleasant oath. As though she had heard him, the girl groaned and half-turned on the bed. Boysie's first recognition. She had been among those in the *au pair* file in Mostyn's office. Blonde. Twenty-three years old. Helmuson. Or was it Holmusen? Something like that. Greta – that was the christian name. He was sure that was the christian name. He let the cover slip back into place. Swinging like a pendulum making tiny scraping noises.

Boysie needed only a brief look into the second cell. His hand shot up for the key. The locked turned easily, the hinges were well oiled.

'Boysie!' said Petronella jumping from the bed.

'Oakes. Well done.' From Lynne. She looked different. The same clothes: cream skirt, sweater and ankle socks. Yet something had changed in her manner. Tigerish.

'You two all right?' said Boysie stupidly.

'Now we're all right. I thought they'd killed you.' Petronella made it sound as though it mattered. By this time, Boysie had slipped into the habit of glancing over his shoulder every few seconds. Jittery.

'Come on then. We'll have to move. There's a girl in the other cell, but she's in no condition...'

'We'll have to leave her then,' snapped Lynne. 'Ruthlessness. We all knew what to expect on this assignment.'

'Oh yes,' said Boysie nearly asking 'What assignment?' He was disturbed by the rabbit Lynne's quick change to the snake Lynne. He might even be losing his natural superiority.

'Follow me then,' trying to make it sound confident. They had gone only a few paces – about to turn into the main passage from the hall when the bell started ringing. A violent, urgent, electric, warning burr. Boysie faltered. Petronella bumped him. Lynne was to their right.

'Run!' hissed Lynne as one of the Seniors sprang into the corridor and leaped towards her. Boysie flailed out with his right hand, but the girl had already closed with Lynne, teeth bared like an animal.

'Run,' Lynne's voice screaming as she backed back against the wall, clawing for her attacker's face.

Angela appeared, steadying herself against the passage wall, coming from her room full tilt. Further down, the other doors were opened – girls crowding out. Angela heading straight for Boysie. For a wonderful second he was inspired.

'Look out,' he yelled. 'Look out, Angela, your pants are coming down.'

With automatic feminine reaction the girl made a grab at her bikini briefs, letting out a yelp of dismay.

It gave them only a couple of seconds advantage, but Boysie was off up the main passageway dragging Petronella in his wake. He could hear the sound of feet close behind. Then a jerk and Petronella was pulled from his grip. He glanced back. Angela had tackled her low down on the knees, and the two girls were sprawled across the passage – an obstacle to the half-a-dozen Seniors who were pelting after them.

'Go on, Boysie. Run. Go on,' yelled Petronella. Boysie faltered for a moment, then the instinct of self-preservation took hold and he was going lickerty-spit up the passage. It was only a matter of seconds before he heard noises from ahead. They were coming from the main building – from the villa. Closing in on both sides. He had reached the gymnasium by this time. The class had finished and the gym looked deserted.

Boysie's shoulder hit the swing doors and he slewed into the great amphitheatre-like hall. At the far end, flanked by wall-bars, were more double doors. He half-ran, half-skated on his bare feet across the polished floor, through the doors and into another small gymnasium. Here, the floor was covered with fibre mats. Racks of foils, épées, sabres and quarterstaves ran the length of the wall to his right. More fencing equipment hung along the other. Mary Van Bracken, in a hugging white track suit, stood in his path.

'Hi!' said Boysie, breathless and trying to look unconcerned. 'Can't find my way out of this maze.'

Mary Van B grinned. 'I don't think you're really meant to get out.'

'Ah,' said Boysie, playing it dim.

She laughed. 'Aren't you the cause of all that noise back there?'

'Well. Yes, but if you'll just let me..'

'Have at you then,' said Miss Van Bracken,

quietly making a jump for the rack of quarterstaves.

Boysie just managed to anticipate, flinging himself in the same direction as the girl. He tried to reach the staff she was tugging from the wall, missed, corrected and grabbed a weapon for himself.

They were solid, seven-foot lengths of oak, smooth to the touch and about as thick as a punt pole. Mary had leaped away into the centre of their home-made tilt-yard, holding her staff, like a rifle and bayonet, in the *en guard* position, its end aimed straight for Boysie's wilting stomach. She was grinning. Irrationally, Boysie thought she looked a bit like Paul McCartney. The hair was the same anyway.

Boysie was gripping his staff in both hands, holding it straight in front of his body. He tried to remember how Errol Flynn had done it in that *Robin Hood* movie. The couple circled each other – Mary's eyes darting around Boysie's body, searching for a suitable target.

'Look, Mary...' Boysie started. She came in with a couple of feints to the left, then a series of quick jabs aimed at the stomach – vicious little prods, with the end of her staff. Boysie retreated. He could hear movements behind him, by the door. Mary shouted, 'No leave him. He's mine.'

'Leave them alone.' Klara's voice. An order.

As they circled again, Boysie was conscious of a group of girls round Klara standing in the doorway. Mary was at him again, pushing forward. Boysie banged down hard. The force of staff against staff hurt his wrists. Again. Again. Finally he knocked the girl's weapon to one side. She took a step back, recovered and flicked her staff into the same position as Boysie's, returning to the attack. Once more they crossed, Boysie giving way a little, the girl consolidating by pressing blows to the centre of his staff, between the hands. Boysie bent his elbows and really took the offensive, using a paddling movement, beating at Mary's staff first with one end, then the other.

She was tiring he could hear her breathing – little panting snorts. He forced on. Then, as Mary raised her quarterstaff above her head for a final assault, he flung his weapon to one side and reached up, hands grasping Mary's staff close to her hands. A twist to the right – still gripping the staff – turning. They were back to back, each still clutching the staff. Boysie bent forward and pulled down with his arms. He felt the girl somersault over his back and watched as she executed a neat twist to land on her feet.

Boysie was pleased with this rather flamboyant move. Too pleased. It took almost three seconds for it to dawn on him that Mary Van Bracken was still hanging on to the quarterstaff. *She* was supposed to let go. *He* should have hung on. Three seconds were too long. Van Bracken had allowed the staff to slide out between her hands. Now, clutching it like an outsize baseball bat she brought it round in a great arc. The first blow caught him on the side of the neck. He did not even feel the second. A flash of light turning to a pinpoint in the whirling darkness. The roar of the sea and then the gabble of voices. He was being pulled to his feet. Dragged and pummelled. The sea began to get rough and, though he used all his concentration, Boysie could not hear the gulls. It was terribly important.

'Whatyer done with all the bloody seagulls,' he shouted.

CHAPTER NINE

GREY SENIORS: BRISSAGO-LONDON

Two score violins – lush and syrupy – were playing an oldie he knew quite well, though he could not put a name to it. The world slushed unevenly back into his brain, though he was not quite sure whether he really wanted it. Cautiously, Boysie opened one eye. For the second time in twenty-four hours he was regaining consciousness. Getting to be a habit. From the prone position he knew immediately that this was going to be worse than last time. He ached horribly. His head, last year's model, seemed somehow detached – a replica moulded from cold scrambled eggs. A nasty thumping pain in his right shoulder, and he could not move properly.

'I'm paralysed,' he said weakly.

'Ah, Boysie's back in the land of the living.' Klara's voice. He moved his head. A pair of polished boots sank into the carpet by his face. He looked higher. Klara Thirel was up there at about 20,000 feet smiling pleasantly. She stepped back. 'Welcome to the party, Boysie. Have a drink.' She was clutching a glass in one hand and a swishy black riding crop in the other. 'Sit him up, girls.'

Boysie moved his head again. Two steam engines came to life, and the Simplon Express made a detour through his cerebellum. Angela and her room mate (back in the grey shirts and short-shorts) lifted him. He was not paralysed but his arms were somehow pinioned to his sides. The girls certainly knew their stuff – points of weight and all that. He was being carried like a baby and plumped into a chair – straps across his chest to the back. Unresisting, he felt straps going round his ankles. He raised his chin from the slumped position. The Simplon Express decided to whistle. Boysie shook his head. He was sure something from inside was spraying out of his ears. Lynne and Petronella were strapped to their chairs on the other side of the room. Quiet. Not struggling. It seemed to be a large office, only the walls would not stop undulating long enough for a close inspection. Some red velvet. Crimson velvet. A desk the size of a billiard table. Above it an oil painting. Klara.

An oil painting of Klara. On the desk, gramophone records and an aged gramophone. Boysie concentrated. The gramophone was providing the singing strings.

'It's *Laura*,' said Boysie happily, recognising the tune.

'That's it, Boysie. *Laura*. One of my favourites. Listen, it's one of their best.' Klara seated herself on the desk on a gleeful attitude. 'Get Boysie a drink, Angela. Do you like French 75s? That's what we're drinking. French 75s.'

Boysie closed his eyes and nodded. This was ridiculous. A great big stupid Cinerama-type dream. Angela came towards him (she managed very well on a floor that kept tilting). The tall blonde slid into his lap, one arm going round his neck, a pair of soft buttocks lowering themselves gently on to his thighs.

'There we are, Boysie. Nice drinkies.' Angela, all intimate and cosy, putting the glass to his lips. The ultra-sophisticated champagne cocktail that is a French 75 went down in one.

'More,' said Boysie.

'Greedy.' Angela leaned forward and touched his cheek with her lips. At that moment the gramophone erupted. *Laura* was just discernible – the melodic line being played at speed on a euphonium. There was a banjo in there as well. Pistol shots and a whole mad razamataz of noise. Then the singer began, with sound effects filling out the lyrics.

'*O Laura* (wolf whistle)
Is the face in the misty light (scream)
Footsteps that you hear down the hall (clump-clump-clump)
The laugh that floats on a summer night.'
    (Maniacal guffaw.)

Klara was rolling about. Angela giggled.
    'Aren't they the end?'
    'I remember them,' said Boysie, still numb. 'From way back I remember them. Spike Jones.'
    'You've got it, Boysie. Spike Jones and his City Slickers. These are my originals. I had them just after I first came here. Someone found a whole box of records in a crashed British truck just across the frontier, in Italy. Spike Jones and his City Slickers. The first real exploiters of popular sick music. The rage when you were fighting my father.'
    'Your father?' Boysie caught her up on the last two words. 'What's your father got to do

with it?' Spike Jones and his hilarious hardware orchestra of the forties brought *Laura* to a cacophonous finale.

'What?' Klara incredulous. 'You know who I am surely, Boysie? Your organisation isn't as badly informed as that. After all you've been trying to make us close shop for the last two years.'

'I know who you are,' spat Lynne. 'Answer no questions, Oakes.'

'Oh shut up,' shouted Boysie. He was getting bored with Lynne's new confidence. Petronella just sat still looking pretty. Klara stood up, the riding crop slapping her right boot with some force.

'I think you'd better leave us, girls.'

Angela rose with a little twitch of her bottom, long fingers giving Boysie's neck a gentle squeeze. Her partner stepped from behind Lynne's chair.

'Hector,' said Angela cryptically.

'Oh my god, where's the stupid thing gone. I was enjoying myself so much.' Klara genuinely distraught. 'He should be back in his nest. It's not really warm enough for him to be out for very long.' She glanced towards the wall near Boysie's chair. About three inches from the floor there was an oblong recess, lit from behind. It was obviously the home of some tropical animal. A thermostat control speared up at one end, and the box was cut off from the room by a sliding glass panel, now three-quarters open. A small ramp led down to the carpet.

'Hector,' purred Klara. 'Hector. Come on, Hector. I'll tempt him out. Ingrid, his food.'

Ingrid (Angela's friend) did not move. She had flattened herself against the wall, her face chalk-white.

'She's no good. Frightened of him.' Angela moved carefully across the room to the desk and picked up a box from behind the gramophone. She handed it to Klara.

'I'm sorry, Principal.' Ingrid was trembling, still trying to push her back through the Sanderson's Silk Finish. 'I'd forgotten he was out. I just can't...'

Klara took no notice. 'Come on, Hector. Nice grasshoppers.'

Petronella screamed. An indrawn shriek of genuine revulsion. Boysie's skin tingled, his veins turning into ant runs and stomach contracting with a slow crawling sensation. Moving slowly over Petronella's feet was a spider. His fear of spiders, he knew, was irrational, but this was too much for anyone. The spider was the largest he had ever seen – a body the size of a medium orange, the head almost as big as a table-tennis ball. It was covered all over with a kind of black plush, its long creeping legs the thickness of a chicken's wishbone. He automatically pressed back into the chair, even though the creature was on the other side of the room.

It spotted Klara and went into a canter.

'There you are. Good boy. Isn't he beautiful?' She offered the beast a dry-looking grasshopper on the palm of her hand, and, as the brute approached, she flicked the titbit into its nest. The spider scuttled past Boysie and up the ramp – he could hear its legs drumming on the wood like a couple of tiny horses. Klara went over, slid the glass panel into place and clicked a small padlock.

'I had to have a lock fitted.' Sounding like a housewife discussing the new dog kennel. 'He's so strong. Used to push the glass open. He loves to come up on to my desk and play with the papers while I'm working.' She smiled affectionately at the revolting Hector who was now demolishing the luckless grasshopper.

Boysie felt nothing but a deep loathing. Ingrid looked as though she was recovering from mild shock.

'You are squeamish, aren't you?' said

193

Klara. 'Hector wouldn't hurt a fly. Well, that's not exactly true, but he certainly wouldn't hurt you.' She turned to Boysie. 'One of my old girls gave him to me. He comes from Brazil.'

'Oh. Where the nuts come from.'

'Indian children there keep them as pets. Even take them around on leads like dogs. They're harmless, friendly things.'

Boysie swallowed and tried to act unconcerned. 'Is he house trained?' Looking shiftily at the spider behind its safety curtain of glass.

Klara laughed. 'All right, girls. I'll call you when I need you.'

Angela and Ingrid both came to attention, doing a smart about turn and leaving the room. Klara was standing directly in front of Boysie. She paused for a moment, the little whip thwacking gently on to the palm of her left hand. At last she spoke quietly.

'You really don't know who I am?'

There were so many paradoxes about the woman. One moment, as now, she could look distinctly desirable; the next, she was a strange, warped person who dispensed sadistic discipline, listened to incongruous nostalgic Spike Jones records, and kept a horrible hairy beast as a gooey woman would keep a Pekinese. Boysie felt tired and not too happy with his stomach.

'Does it really matter, Doctor Thirel?'

'It matters to me.' She was still speaking softly, but with a hint of fire in her eyes. 'And I think it matters to you. You haven't been briefed properly, dear Boysie. Lynne, as she calls herself, knows who I am. It worries me that you do not.'

'Look, this isn't a plot. I'm not implicated in any Machiavellian plan. I haven't really got anything to do with Lynne. My head aches, I feel sick; and if it's all the same to you I'd rather call it a day.'

Klara nodded. 'And if you're not implicated with Sweet Lynne why did you come running so quickly when she invited you to the *Madonna Del Sasso?* An invitation which, you will have guessed, I intercepted.' A bleak, thin rearrangement of the lips. 'Let's try your reflexes.' The riding crop flicking her hand again.

'Oh hell,' moaned Boysie to himself, 'now we're going to get the rough stuff.'

'Thirel. That's your first clue. I'm rather proud of it as an anagram.'

Boysie's mind began to make mechanical fumbles with the letters – Thelir, Lireth, Ethril. He gave up after Ethril.

'I was brought here twenty years ago.' Klara, determined to have her say. 'A girl with very fixed ideas. This place – the villa and the underground shelters – had been bought in my name as early as 1940. At least my parents made sure that I was taken care of.' A ghost laugh. Cynical. 'They were making sure for themselves as well mind you. *Il Portone* was supposed to be a bolt hole. A rat hole. A hidey hole. I got here on April 26th, 1945. A great friend of my father was due to arrive a few days later. He never made it – him and the woman. Caught and shot on Lake Como on the 28th.' Her feet were apart, hands clasped together in front of her round the whip. 'Two days later, in a Berlin bunker my mother was poisoned and my father shot himself.' The eyes holding Boysie like little magnetic rays. 'Now do you know?'

Boysie was too mushy with fatigue to take in the enormity of what Klara was saying. He stared hard trying to superimpose a picture over Klara's face. The picture of a grim face with hard eyes; a lock of hair falling forward on the forehead; an absurd moustache.

'But...'

Klara nodded again. 'It's true Boysie.

Most of the European Press have speculated for years. The few people who know have kept quiet. Some as the – need I finish the cliché?'

Boysie wanted to shout and throw things around. But, when he spoke, the words just about made it.

'So you've been carrying on the good work. Subversive super-women. Neo-bleeding-Nazis.'

The final word seemed to trigger a vast hidden supply of passion. Klara's face flushed a furious red; her hands clenching and unclenching as if trying to master some terrible upflow of temper. When she spoke, her voice quavered on the borderline of sanity.

'No. You don't know.' A whistling intake of breath. 'When my father and mother died I could have danced on their bodies. I had neither seen nor spoken to them for eight years – and I don't suppose they were over anxious to see me. But I was useful.' Two more beats with the riding crop. Another intake of breath. 'Since the day that man died I have done everything possible to help those most diametrically opposed to him.' She spun on a booted hell, marched back to the desk, rooting among the pile of records, slipping one on to the old gramophone and cranking the winding handle. Spike Jones blared out again – ribald and very much from the past. Boysie remembered his own inconspicuous and unheroic part in the war to end all wars against Klara's father. The barrack rooms and blackout pubs. The comic radio shows. Tommy Handley. Be like Dad keep Mum. The background to the times when he was a NAAFI cowboy. An ATS girl's knees. Somebody thumping out tunes on a jangling piano. *Yours, Room 504, That Lovely Weekend, We're Going to Hang Out the Washing on the Siegfried Line,* and this song rising from the dead era.

> '*When der Fuhrer says we is der master race,*
> *Then we*
> *Heil! (Pharp)*
> *Heil! (Pharp)*
> *Right in der Fuhrer's face.*'

After each 'Heil' a relishing rude raspberry parping out of the loudspeaker. Lynne's little face looked set and frozen. Petronella was bewildered, anxious. The record ground on.

'That's what I think of him and his wretched memory and his accursed ideas,' shouted Klara from the desk. 'That's all I think of him.'

'Well, if not Neo-Nazi then certainly subversive super-women,' Boysie shouted back.

The record half-echoed:

'Are we not der supermen?
Aryan pure supermen?
Are we not der supermen?
Super-duper-duper-men.'

Boysie recalled Angela.

'You should know. Your people have been trying to put me out of business for the last two years. Girl after girl you've infiltrated and not one of them's lasted more than a fortnight.' The voice rising like a shrike on the wing. 'And what are you here for, Boysie? Heavy stuff? A blaster to crush us? Are you people so frightened of the best women's training centre in Europe?'

The record finished: the old round gramophone head swinging backwards and forwards with a regular clicking noise. Boysie felt marked regrets at not having jacked in the job years ago. Lynne spoke.

'And what are you going to do with us now Fraulein Schicklgruber?'

Boysie closed his eyes and winced, expecting the riding crop to whisk across the girl's shoulders. But Klara was in full control.

'I have no doubts about you, my pet,' she said, firm and ugly, straight at Lynne. 'If I had my way you'd be mutton at the bottom of the lake now. Just like the last idiot child you sent.'

Petronella rocked her head to and fro.

'However,' continued Klara, 'after that episode I have been instructed to refer everything to those whom I assist.' She turned towards Boysie. 'Neither am I completely certain about your comrade Oakes, or your friend Petronella. So I must wait for orders.' She leaned forward, balancing the weighted end of the whip, pointing at Lynne. 'You already have some insight into the fact that another branch of our service is using our premises for an experiment.'

'Amber Nine.' Lynne. Unemotional.

'For want of a better name.' Klara moved her thumb up and down. The end of the whip rose and fell. 'Because of this we are incommunicado.'

'Radio silence,' said Boysie trying to be helpful. Pleased with himself at remembering one of his Department's code sequences. Klara looked at him suspiciously. 'Until tomorrow night.' She finished. Leaning back over the desk she picked up the telephone and spoke rapidly.

'Send Angela and her group up here at once.' Returning the instrument to its cradle. 'So, my dears, until tomorrow night I must keep you close mew'd up – as the English poet has it. The only problem is, who will sleep with who? Or should it be whom?' A pleasant grin, her eyes sweeping the three faces. Then, decisively: 'Let's have some more of Mr Spike Jones and his City Slickers.'

The record was somewhat sick. A little number entitled *My Old Flame*, in which a gentleman giving a splendid impression of Peter Lore bewails the fact he cannot remember his old flame's name ('I'll have to look through my collection of human heads'). No one else has ever been the same ('They won't even let me strangle them'). Klara was laughing fit to split her girdle.

'Life with Klara,' thought Boysie wearily, 'was just one chuckle after another.'

The Chief's Silver Shadow turned into the Mall. The rain had stopped just before midnight, leaving the road a wide grey mirror streaked with irregular splurges of yellow from the street lamps. The Chief of the Department of Special Security had been in many tight corners during his tempestuous life. If it was not for the Official Secrets Act he might have written a remarkable auto-biography. In one of his more egotistical moments he had even drafted a first chapter and title – *From the High Seas to High Places*. The chapter began: 'I was born a child of fortune...'

Now, the Chief tried to look reality steadily in the eyes. It was bad enough in the Navy, but the responsibilities of Security were beginning to take their toll on his leather mind and body. At this particular moment, surrounded by all the smooth luxury of a Rolls Royce, he felt undeniably dodgy. It was difficult to recall a time when he had felt so dodgy. Perhaps during the Russian convoys. Or maybe that night at the Savoy when his wife telephoned and the soubrette (pre-viously fourth on the bill at Collins Music Hall) had answered. 'Charmin' girl,' thought the Chief. 'Delightful way of...' He pulled his reluctant mind back to matters in hand. It was late, and the Director of Supreme Control had been more than acid over the telephone.

'Chief of Special Security?' The unmistakable gravelled, gruff voice through the earpiece – the instrument clutched for on the verge of sleep.

'Yes.' The Chief was not fully awake.

'DSC. I'm calling an immediate conference – all Chiefs of Departments.'

The Chief looked at his watch. 'At this time of…?'

'Immediate.' The line went dead, as though the DSC had exploded in a little shower of irritability.

A sudden conference of Chiefs of Departments was as extraordinary as a Beatles concert in the Wigmore Hall. There were, of course, the biannual get-togethers in Dorset; and Departmental heads expected to be called upon from time to time. But a crash meeting like this was unnerving: boding shake-ups, Royal Commissions, talk of mismanagement of duties – public funds even. It was all very disturbing, and could only mean one thing. Somewhere, someone had blundered horribly; and the Chief knew that events during the previous day pointed to a rapid rise in clanger-dropping – some of it heading nastily near home. Really, he mused, this should not come as a surprise. Her Majesty's Security Service – like all military and government departments – was an unwieldly and disseminated organisation. Countless tightening projects failed to undermine the staunch conservative attitudes existing in the executive of what is now Britain's front-line weapon in the cold war. To begin with, there is the major headache of an establishment administered partly by Service personnel and partly by members of the Civil Service, Home and Foreign Offices.

A dozen central departments – including MI5, MI6, Special Branch, Management and Support Intelligence and Special Security – had expanded over the years. Throwing off minor shoots. Creating new branches. For the Director of Supreme Control (the Chief often thought) the job of co-ordinating the whole complex must be a nightmare. That was probably why Special Security was seldom worried by directives from the Top. While the surface remained reasonably unruffled the DSC preferred to stay in his ivory tower. Most people kept their jobs that way. Yet when you looked at it objectively, it was obvious. Department over-lapped department; the terms of reference of one branch fell right across those of another; the red tape of section A was constantly ravelled with the blue tape of section B. As a Chief of Department it was usually better to ignore these things: leave them to the underlings. But sometimes..? Was the DSC's sudden night call the harbinger of a complete breakdown? The start of a ruthless weeding out? The Chief thought sadly about some of the things concerning his own department. Particularly the way his Second-in-Command managed to cut corners and get rid of security risks by employing a liquidating agent. If the truth about that one got out it would be curtains – velvet with gold fringes. The name Penton kept coming into the Chief's mind.

The Rolls slid to a silent halt. Already five other Silver Shadows were parked outside the building. McBronstien, the chauffeur, opened the door, and the Chief of the Department of Special Security stepped out, heading for trouble.

'Bum,' said Boysie dangerously, as the cell door thumped and the key clunked in the lock. Klara's office was situated in the underground warren off the small gymnasium in which Boysie had fought his first, and last, quarterstaff battle. They were marched stiffly (the straps had played havoc with Boysie's circulation) back to the cells by Angela and six Seniors – the blonde Ingrid trying to look menacing with Boysie's Sauer & Sohn. Lynne, silent and thin-lipped, was pushed into the lock-up already containing the injured Helmuson (or was it Holmusen?) girl. 'She'll be all right,' said Klara looking at the flayed back with indifference. 'I've examined her and she'll live. For the time being anyway.'

Boysie and Petronella were waved into the other cell. It was at this point that Boysie, with some feeling, said 'Bum.'

'Bum,' echoed Petronella in key with Boysie's sentiments.

'Arse.'

'Arse.'

'Sh...'

'Oh, shshsh, Boysie.' Petronella came close, put a hand over his mouth and stepped away. 'That woman. My god, when I get my hands on that woman.' Quivering, motivated not by the earlier tears, but by stark rage. 'I'll screw the pants off her when I get her.'

'Good for you.' Boysie waking up to the fact of Petronella's womanhood. He had been struck by her physical charms before

206

the whole wretched catastrophe erupted. Yet, subconsciously, he had decided that she was not really his type. All that crying. As though reading his thoughts, Petronella spoke.

'Sorry if I've been a bit willowy, Boysie. I'm all right now.'

Boysie nodded. His forgiving smile. 'I'll say.'

'It's all been so odd. And Karen's death. Well, it's not like me to go under.'

'Really?'

'Yes, really.' Sharp. A hand to her head. Fingers furrowing through the rich red waves. 'Now, what the hell are we going to do about it? I don't really understand what's going on, but...'

Boysie looked at Petronella, dishevelled but unequivocally gorgeous, leaning against the cell wall, her thighs hard against her dress, the breasts trying to force their way through the silk. He looked at the bed, then realised he was in no shape for acrobatics. It had been a hard, tough day. His head still felt cracked, he was getting mild double vision and there was an uncomfortable niggly pain under the left second rib. Incongruously, Boysie remembered his annual X-ray was just about due. At his age, he argued, you could not be too careful. He looked at the bed again.

'You take the bed, Petronella, old love. I'll be OK on the floor.'

She smiled, moved her hand to the back of the dress and downwards. There was the soft metallic tearing sound of a zip. The dress fell from her left shoulder. Then the right. Skin like vanilla ice cream. Boysie forced a wan grin.

'There's room for both of us, Boysie. Easily room for both.'

Fatigue washed over Boysie like a cold shower. He was also conscious that, in spite of Petronella's charms, his essential virility felt as if it had been the victim of a heavy cocaine injection. He would never manage in this state.

'Come on, Boysie, get undressed.'

'No, really, you have the bed.' Boysie, vainly proud of his normal prowess, faced humiliation.

Petronella laughed. A tinkle, as though at some private joke. 'It's all right, love. I only want someone to cling to. I need to feel someone close.' Her dress slipped to the floor. Hope loomed in the shape of Mary Quant underwear, the black and white Lycra elastic panties which (Boysie knew to his chagrin) could be as manproof as armour plating.

Petronella giggled. 'Sorry if I egged you on.' Crossing to the bed. There was no getting away from it, she had splendid thighs – the full silken bit. 'Naughty. Forgive me. But I'm not a man's girl, Boysie. For me it's jolly hockey sticks.' Blatant. 'Why do you think I was so upset about Karen? She was much more than a step-sister to me. Sorry. Come on. Come to bed, feller.'

Relief wandered gently through Boysie's nervous system. He looked about him for the light switch. None. Shrugging, he stripped to his jockeys briefs and slid into the narrow bed beside Petronella.

'There'll be a way out,' he said, trying to convince himself. 'Tomorrow, there'll be a way out.'

Petronella wrapped her arms round him and they both closed their eyes. Paradoxically, the sense of exhaustion flowed out of him – the old familiar urges tingling censorable messages to nerves, and from nerves to arteries.

'A couple of hundred birds within easy reach.' He sighed. 'A couple of hundred pacey little pussycats, dollies, judies, sheilas, birds. And I have to get shacked up with a

Les.' Still pondering on the injustice of life, he dropped slowly, and insecurely, into a sleep etched with somewhat lurid dreams.

Mostyn cursed the telephone bell and switched on the light, glancing at his watch. Four-thirty in the morning. It was the red extension. His night line to the Chief.

'Number Two?'

Mostyn was wide awake. The Chief's voice had a humid pre-storm, cumulonimbus texture.

'Number Two here.'

'Ah. Sleepin' at HQ. Guilty conscience?'

He knew it had been a bad decision to sleep at headquarters. The Chief was bound to make something out of it. The old boy picked up things like that. Worked on them.

'What's up, Chief?'

'The balloon, little Mostyn. Been at a meetin' with the DSC since one o'clock this bleedin' mornin'.'

'Oh I say, that's a bit thick.'

'More'n a bit thick Almost bloody solidified.' The Chief snarled – a deplorable sign. 'Been trying to save our skins, Number Two.'

Mostyn took a deep breath. Essential to

remain calm. 'What seems to have happened?'

'Nothin' seems. It has. Better come up. I'm in me office.' There was a clink of bottle-neck against glass rim from the Chief's end. 'In the meantime, ever come across Strategic Intelligence?'

Mostyn set his thought processes in motion. 'Vaguely. Small off-shoot of MI6 aren't they? Boffins. Keep themselves to themselves.'

'Ah. Keep them-bloody-selves to them-bloody-selves. That's the fun of this game, Laddie. Let not they left hand know what they right hand's doin'. Boffins. Bunch o' queers. Long-haired- perverts. No doubt.' A gulping noise like whisky being poured down a petrified throat. 'Goin' to need a damn good story, Mostyn. Be one hell of a probe over this one. Precious Strategic flamin' Intelligence've embarked on a rotten great operation without tellin' anybody. Right in the middle of one of our areas. Even got NATO assistance. And we knew nothin'!'

'Someone's head...'

'Will roll. Yes. You tamperin' around with Wheater and Thirel. Askin' all those questions. It's brought lord knows what out into the open. Everyone's been caught with their drawers at half mast.' The Chief paused for a grim little chortle. 'Specially Trainin' Command. My God, they've got an almighty 'orrible secret up their filthy sweaty sleeves. Turn your hair grey. Talk about our problems. Wouldn't like to be in those beetle-crushers Chief of Training Command wears.'

Mostyn shook his head. Three or four large bats had taken flight between his ears. The Chief was off again, skidding the conversation in another direction.

'Let's get this straight. You sent Oakes on an assignment?'

'You know I did.'

'All right. Just bein' methodical. The Penton assignment?'

'Yes.'

'Back in the saddle. His old job.'

Gloomily. 'Yes.'

'You know where he is? Where "L" is?'

'Ah.' Ambiguous.

'Well?'

'Well, roughly. Roughly where he is.'

'Not good enough, Number Two. Roughly is no good. I want to know where he is exactly. Map bloody reference. Latitude and longitude. Compass bearin'. Pinpoint.

Radio fix. Whatd'y last hear?'

'He was in the Locarno area and he'd gone out with a young woman...'

'Might've known.'

'Called Whitching. Petronella Whitching. Step-sister of the Schport girl – one that was drowned.'

'Womanisin'. Fornicatin' all over mountainsides. That the way for people to behave? At it in chalets? Makin' each other in ski-lifts?'

'No, Chief.'

'No. Had he met the Thirel woman? Actually met her?'

'Yes.'

'In the lurid flesh met her?'

'Yes.'

'You think it's likely – even by the longest stretch – is it likely that he's gone out to her blasted school.'

'Hard to say.' Evasive, sensing the danger.

'On the cards?'

'Definitely on the cards...'

'Why?'

'She invited him. Out to the school she invited him. Told me. It's in the sub-text of his telephone conversation.'

'The one with you? When he mentioned Wheater and all that?'

'Yes.'

'You got the tape handy? Bring it up when you come. He'd been invited. Christ. And Martin?'

'Won't have arrived yet, sir.'

'Better get up here at the smart run, Mostyn. Think I've pulled the blinkers over most people's eyes. Got permission for you to go out and represent us because this bloody Strategic Intelligence is operatin' in our area. Give you all the 'orrible truth up here. There'll be a Royal Commission on this one sure as eggs have little lions. God save our necks. Always said there was no liaison. Nobody knows what the hell anyone else is up to. Whole organisation operates like a blasted civil war. Prime Minister's shouting blue, black and green murder. Says nobody ever tells him anything.' Another clink. 'Get up 'ere. Too late to stop Strategic Intelligence, but this could be another U-2 scandal. Oh my merciful sainted aunt. Think I'll go on leave once I've packed you off.'

In the Chief's office – chill in the early hours – Mostyn listened to a tale of snowballing intrigue which cast long and dark shadows. He was particularly worried about his own job at Special Security. As the Chief

214

talked, so Mostyn reacted with mounting anxiety. Right in the middle of things Training Command and Strategic Intelligence were amalgamated in an historic conspiracy. Poised over the bubbling pot was 'L' – Brian Ian (Boysie) Oakes.

'It would have to be our boy,' said Mostyn sounding like a man eager to resign before the fraud squad got their hands on the company accounts. 'It would have to be him. On neutral territory well. And you know how he can blot copy books.'

'*Your* copy book,' said the Chief. Then, being realistic for once. 'And ultimately mine. However much I lie, ultimately mine.'

'I'll do what I can.'

'I know you will, old chap. I know.' An arm on Mostyn's shoulder. 'Shouldn't bother to come back if you don't...'

Mostyn sighed.

'Go and get organised then, little Mostyn. Commercial to Zürich. We've got clearance after that for a helicopter down to Monte Ceneri – the Maggiore airfield. Can't take Jets. Should be in Locarno by midday.'

'Get Martin to meet me.' Mostyn's eyes narrowed. Nasty, short-lashed slits. 'And if

Oakesie's made a balls. If he's got us involved in anything...' There was no need to go on.

CHAPTER TEN

SCARLET SUNRISE:
LAKE MAGGIORE

Now they were trying to suffocate him. Were there no lengths to which these women would go? Boysie threshed around and came soaring back to consciousness, grabbing at the hand pressed hard against his mouth.

'Shut up, Oakes. Quiet.'

He opened his eyes and looked up at Lynne Wheater whose palm was forced against his teeth. She was becoming a proper little dictatoress. Boysie stopped struggling. Lynne removed her hand putting a finger to her lips.

'How the...?' Boysie screwed the sleep out of his eyes and looked past Lynne. The cell door was open – part of a female leg just visible, lying twisted on the passage floor. Boysie turned. Petronella was still floating through dreams peopled with girls like herself. Lynne held Boysie's Sauer &

Sohn, not pointing it at anything in particular.

'How did you…?'

'Thirel is not omnipotent.' Low. Almost a whisper, a wager of smile crossing her mouth. 'We infiltrated Ingrid eighteen months ago. Undetected, but she needed help. That's why we've been trying to get girls in.'

'Who're you with?'

'I was going to ask you the same question.' The Sauer & Sohn came up, an inch from Boysie's nose.

'Special Security.' No point in hedging.

Lynne wrinkled her brow. 'I've never worked with any of your people.'

'And you?'

'Assault One.'

'Oh yes.' He had never heard of Assault One, but in this business it did not mean a thing.

'Ingrid has shown me the way. We can be with the others in half-an-hour.'

'The others.' Boysie nodded. Lost. Anything to be out of Klara's reach. Keeping the blanket round him for the sake of decency, he stretched out for his shirt. Lynn handed it over.

'Did you get any message through?

Through to Wheater? To the Wimbledon number?'

'Your control?' Casual. Very pro.

'Mm-hu.'

'I sent it through *my* control.'

'Good. Good.'

Boysie was climbing out of the bed trying not to let Lynne see his underwear. He knew how girls felt getting out of sports cars. Petronella rolled over.

'You were taking a risk weren't you?' he said. 'Getting me to phone Wheater. You didn't know me. What if I'd been the opposition?'

'The risk was calculated. It worked didn't it?' She motioned the gun towards Petronella. 'What about her?'

'*What* about her?'

'Isn't she with you?'

'Not really.'

'She said she was with you. When we were locked in here – before you turned up, and all that Spike Smith…'

'Jones.'

'…Jones business. She said she was with you.'

'She was. When they got me. Stumbled into it. The Schport girl's step-sister.'

'Better take her along, you think?'

'Of course,' Boysie, pulling on his trousers. 'You're not what I thought.'

'No?'

'No. All mousey and downtrodden at the hotel. When Klara and her two hoods were after you. Or should it be snoods? Female hoods?'

'We are taught to act. Assault One has some good actresses.'

They woke Petronella – grumbling at first, then speedy and excited at the thought of freedom. Before leaving the cell Boysie took charge of the pistol – loaded, magazine full, safety-catch off.

'We go straight along the Seniors' corridor and through the door at the very end. It leads to the bathrooms. There are steps from there up to the island,' whispered Lynne.

Outside the cell door a ginger-headed Senior sprawled across the passage, her neck twisted to one side, lip pulled back in a set, and very unfunny, grin. They had to step over the body. Boysie swallowed and gave a disgusted look. Petronella went light grey.

'Ingrid?' asked Boysie with a nod towards the corpse. Lynne signified an affirmative. 'She's very good with necks.'

220

Boysie raised his eyebrows.

Ingrid herself was standing outside the door of the room she shared with Angela.

'They're all asleep, but don't make too much noise.' The touch of Italian in her accent seemed more pronounced. 'Good luck.'

They padded down to the door at the end of the passage. Inside it was dark and there seemed to be no windows. Slowly, feeling out with his hands, Boysie moved forward. He was just reaching back, to comfort himself that Lynne was still behind him, when something clammy touched his cheek. He leaped to one side, the pistol up and ready. Another something twined stickily around his neck. A picture of Hector flashed briefly across his mind. If Klara could keep Hector what other monsters might she have hidden away, guarding escape routes?

'Lights. For god's sake, lights.' He tried not to shout.

A click from the doorway. The premature flicker of the strip lights, then the full blaze. Lynne stood by the switch; Petronella by the door. Boysie was immediately below a clothes line from which two brassières, one suspender belt, four pairs of nylons and a couple of unidentifiable female garments drip-dried harmlessly. The suspender belt (black, with attractive blue bows) was curled round Boysie's neck. He stepped to one side, unwinding and trying on a grin.

They were in a large stone wash-house. Three Hoover Keymatics against the far wall. Doors leading into bath cubicles to right and left. Above the washing machines was a large mirror. Boysie pulled himself up squaring his shoulders as his reflection came into view – a hand automatically to his hair. He looked terrible. A quick profile. Still ghastly.

'Come on. Over there. The door,' Lynne pointing to the left of the washing machines.

Three strides and Boysie reached the door, jerking it open and leaping inside, pistol ready to spout in true commando fashion. Unluckily, a flight of steps led straight down to the door, and the act of leaping caused Boysie's feet to connect hard with the second step. He bounced forward, then slithered down in a crestfallen, spreadeagled lump.

'Come on, Oakes. Quickly.' A hand on his shoulder helping him up.

Boysie motioned Petronella up the steps in front of him, taking the middle position for himself. It was a long climb. A reasonably broad stairway at first, gradually narrowing and changing into a tight stone spiral – dimly lit by blue guiding lamps, a rope running through large iron eyes on the right. It was like going up the old church tower when Boysie was a kid – a treat for the choirboys on Easter Sunday, with a view across the village to the edge of the world over the curving green downs once you reached the top. It took ten minutes before Petronella whispered.

'We're coming to a trapdoor.'

'Coming to a trapdoor.' Boysie passed it down to Lynne.

'Well open the wretched thing. Open it.'

'Open it.'

'I'll try.'

Petronella, precariously balanced on a narrow step, reached upwards. Her hemline rose. Boysie's face was level with her heels. He lifted his head to see how she was getting on, but the view was obscured.

'What a waste,' he thought, eyes playing round that which obscured his line of vision. There was the creak of hinges, followed by a bump. Petronella began to move again.

The trapdoor came up through the floor of a round summerhouse, large enough to contain a dozen people with ease – a musty smell, curved wooden seats, little leaded windows through which first light was beginning to crawl. The flagged floor hurt like ice on Boysie's bare feet.

'Damn,' Lynne, waspish and agitated. 'It's later than I thought. Sun will be up soon.' She walked to the door – newly painted, at variance with the dilapidated, crumbling look of the interior – taking a key from her skirt pocket. Ingrid had been thorough. The key turned easily.

'We should be on the south side of the island. Behind the villa.'

'What villa? Not *Il Portone?*' Boysie's bearings all to blazes.

An exasperated noise from Lynne. 'We're on the larger of the two islands. The villa where they have the equipment for the Amber Nine things.'

'Ah.' Knowingly. 'I was going to ask you. What's it all about?'

'Amber Nine? I hoped you'd be able to tell me. Ingrid has nothing on it. But it's big. You have no ideas?'

'Couldn't tell an Amber Nine from a haycart.'

'Don't you think we ought...?' Petronella gently intruding.

'She's right. Plenty of time to talk about Amber Nine later. The path to the left should take us straight down to the boathouse. You first, Oakes.'

'The name's Boysie.'

'Go on.'

It was damp underfoot; a sweet early morning smell coming fresh to the nostrils. Shrubs and foliage on each side of the narrow gravel track obscured any view, but in the half-light Boysie made out the hard angles of a large house rising on their left. Twenty yards down the path – twisting in gentle curves: a lovers' walk – they could hear the faint lap of water. Two cypress trees on the right. A stone ornament. A short column on which rested the head and shoulders of a severe-looking lady with a pleasing bust, tastefully done in stone. A mimosa bush, then out into an open space, the lake in front of them – a small stone jetty with steps leading into the water. Tied to a ring in the steps, rocking gently, was a clean, trim little speedboat. A *Sweet-16* in powder blue. Lynne pushed past Boysie, down the steps, jumping into the boat with an experienced professionalism which could only have been bred at Cowes. Boysie thought what a remarkable young woman she was – looking, in the simple skirt and ankle socks, like a slightly soiled college girl. Yet, underneath there was a flint of purpose. Lynne helped Petronella into the stern seat and positioned herself behind the wheel. Boysie clambered in beside her. The craft rolled doubtfully and then settled.

'Where we going then?' Boysie like a day tripper, twined an arm round Lynne's shoulders, transferring the pistol to his left hand.

'Hope she starts first time,' Lynne's hands checking the controls. 'The group should be set now. On the other side of the lake. The place is between San Nazzaro and Gerra. We'll have to swing round the island, straight across, then cut back. I don't think they'll risk shooting at this time of day. Not so close to the shore.'

It was getting lighter every minute. Boysie could make out the mainland facing them over the short stretch of water – detail emerging like some trick of film: the campanile, huddle of houses and the line of cypresses that was Brissago: *Il Portone*, standing apart, sleeping. He could clearly see the terrace where he had stood with Klara on the previous evening.

'Cast off that rope and keep everything

crossed,' Lynne's right forefinger on the button starter. The rope fell away. Lynne pressed. The starter made a noise like a coy goosed girl. Twice the engine coughed and died. Lynne tried again. This time the full roar. Boysie felt the push of power in the small of his back as the boat leaped forward, Lynne tight on the wheel in a quarter turn as they slid round in an arc of spray.

'I can hardly hold her. God she's nippy.' Yelling above the frenzied roar of the engine and the hiss of water exploding against the bows, Lynne was pushing down on the throttle: opening to maximum revs. Boysie glanced behind him. They were skating across the water leaving a long plume of foam churning in their wake. To the right the sun just coloured the tops of the mountains. On. Bucketing slightly, hitting a swell. The whole mountain range to the east lit from behind by a wide crimson light. It could have been some city, flashed and flushed out by a nuclear horror. Scarlet now bounced off the thin overhang of cloud, then back on to the lake – a huge bowl of blood in a black jagged container – the spray from the bows picking up the colours: tiny flying shreds of indigo, yellow, orange, and the ever-present scarlet.

Now the sun was edging up. Long spears of light climbing the mountains ahead of them. Brissago and the twin islands, behind, caught in a blotch of shadow. The scarlet of sunrise washed away by softer colours – the blue-green of the lake, shades of olive dotted with cream and pink buildings, sprinkled like confetti thrown against the lower slopes. Olive turning to grey, and, finally, into the white of snow hanging on to the tips.

'Yhaa-hoo!' shouted Boysie, clinging on, his arm round Lynne's shoulders, face drenched with spray. This he enjoyed. No sense of fear or impending disaster. Lynne was shouting again.

'I'll head right up the lake, then we'll slow down, turn and go past headquarters – in case they've got the glasses on us from the island. Don't want them to pinpoint.'

Boysie nodded enthusiastically. Lynne whipped the revs higher, the bows moved up a fraction and the far lakeside – four or five kilometres away – drew closer.

Ten minutes later they were cruising gently, about twenty yards from the coast – the Isole di Brissago now only a pair of small lumps far away over the sheen on the lake. The engine note dropped to a steady hum.

'Gerra coming up.' Lynne relaxed at the wheel. 'Look happy.'

'Fun-loving and filthy rich,' Boysie chortling. The relief to be free of Klara and her brood was enormous.

'Whoww,' breathed Petronella.

One or two locals were already about, near the landing pier. A bell clanged out – a magnet for the early mass. Boysie waved – for verisimilitude – as they slid past the village. The coast was rocky, little pebble beaches and sprouts of large stone; trees coming down to within a few paces of the water's edge; the occasional holiday villa, shutters still closed. Up and behind, early drivers sped along the scenic road which runs from Bellinzona right up the lakeside, across the Italian frontier on to Calende and the autostrada which zips into Milan from the north.

'We're coming to it now,' Lynne excited. 'Just round this headland.' The familiar stony beach dotted with shrubs, one low willow trailing in the water, and a villa – built high up, a large boathouse jutting out below the main terrace. It was a strangely un-symmetrical place, a conglomeration of windows, different sizes, shoved into the walls on five levels. An odd variation of colours as well, faded pink and new-licked-green – the bleached red roof repaired, in one place with blue tiles. It looked like some strange creation erected by an eccentric family. As they drew abreast of the building, a pair of French windows opened on to the terrace. They seemed to have opened by themselves, and at first Boysie thought it was a child coming out to look at them. Then his stomach transformed into frozen sago pudding. He felt hungry, sick, tired and world weary all at once. White corpuscles were playing *Danse Macabre* with his nerves.

'The Chief's arrived then,' said Lynne brightly. 'Just in time for the fun. I wonder if he's got any news of Khavichev. You knew Khavichev was ill?'

Boysie had no idea that Khavichev was ill. He did know that Khavichev was Director of Redland's Counterespionage and Subversive Activities. He also knew the man on the terrace – now leaning over the stone balustrade, shading his eyes with one good hand (the other arm was clasped tight to his chest, in a sling). He was dark and very small. Lynne's chief was the dwarf Kadjawaji. He seemed to have a nasty limp as well.

'Looks as though he's been in an accident,' from Lynne.

230

Boysie's reflexes had gone to pieces. He could not breathe properly and there was the thump of fear above his eyes. He looked down. It took thirty seconds to register that he was still holding the pistol.

'Did you know Khavichev was…?' Lynne started to repeat. Then. 'You ill? You look ill, Oakes.'

'Be all right,' grunted Boysie through his teeth, thinking he was going to be very ill. This was the full topsy-turvy land bit. The big nightmare and the screaming habdabs. Right in the wrong boat. They were almost past the villa. No sign that Kadjawaji had recognised him. The breathing eased a little.

'Go on.' Muttered. Still finding difficulty in talking. If he spoke he would be sick. He knew it.

'Not far if you're feeling a bit sick. I know where we can pull in and walk back. There's a track through the bushes to the boathouse door.'

Act now. He had to act now. This minute. But his muscles were not obeying the frantic signals sent out from his brain. The only muscle working was the involuntary twitch on the left of his mouth. The agony of decision. The revolting pause before the leap into space. Like standing on the top board at the school swimming pool ('Garn, Boysie.' "E's bloody afraid to go.' 'Remember what I promised, Boysie' – the Girls' Grammar Junior Netball Captain). His grip tightened around Lynne's shoulder and the left arm slowly came up, the pistol almost touching her neck. There was a tiny mole, he noticed, below the ear. 'Turn away from the shore and head back to the island.' This was not his voice. His words, but not his normal speech. He felt Lynne's body react with a fraction of fear. Beware of the moment of relaxation. (That's when they try something silly. The bald instructor had told him, in Hampshire. When they relax they're going to have a go.)

'Don't do anything Petronella. For Christ's sake don't do anything. Your sister was on the wrong bloody side.' Over his shoulder, hoping Petronella had not get her loyalties mixed.

Pistol right into the neck now. Flesh pulling away as though the muzzle was red hot. 'Come on, Lynne. Fast. Fast across the lake. Move, you bitch. Move.'

A word spat from the girl's mouth. Increased speed. The skin drawn taut over the bone structure of Lynne's face. Femininity disappearing. Hamlet again– 'Now get you to my lady's chamber, and tell her, let her paint an inch thick, to this favour she must come.' Teeth biting into her lip. Faster. Bows coming up. The roar. A tiny smear of blood where a tooth penetrated the flesh.

'Boysie?' Petronella trying to move forward. Then Lynne reacted. A snarling roar of speed and the wheel spinning hard over. All balance gone, Boysie thought he would be thrown out. Vaguely he glimpsed Petronella behind him, her mouth open. Shouting. Clinging on – hair a wild wet ragged stream. A skidding wave of foam as the little speedboat slewed round, propellers shrieking out of the water and then dipping, biting into the spray. Bows aimed straight for the shore. Lynne's knuckles on the wheel, white. Boysie knew he should shoot. Self-preservation told him to shoot. Ordered him. The boat righted itself. A tiny bay ahead. Blurred. Rocks. Like bloody great Henry Moore statues tossed among the pebbles by some giant. He could not pull the blasted trigger. Boysie felt the gun drop from his fingers as he made a dive for Lynne. Her hands leaving the wheel, just as his clenched fist connected. The noise of the clout clipped out above the hysteria of the engine and the wind and water. Rocks rushing towards them. Inflating. Lynne toppling sideways, her head lolling over the starboard gunwale. Boysie grabbed at the wheel and wrenched. Too late. A lurch as their keel struck the shallows. Massive rocks around them. The crunch of fibreglass splitting as the bows crumbled inwards. A force heaved Boysie forward one shoulder hard against the windshield.

Petronella was screaming, and Boysie just saw Lynne's head strike the rock, among the debris – a bursting open, hideous, blood and tissue smeared out over brown stone. Head sheared in half. Another lurch. A last growl as the propellers cracked. Then silence.

'Arse uppards,' Boysie groaned. 'They've all got it arse uppards.' The original shock – Lynne's innocent mention of Khavichev. The resurrection of Kadjawaji. The sudden complete reversal of sides and roles – had blocked out the deeper horror, wrapping it away in a dark untouched pocket of his subconscious.

He dragged the dazed Petronella from the wreckage – retching twice as they stumbled up the beach in the general direction of the road – no definite plan in his addled mind. Grabbing Petronella by the wrist, Boysie yanked her into the bushes. Four paces in (a scratch on his hand; there were some big sharp-pointed leaves) then flat, wishing he could burrow into the earth and shingle. People would be coming any minute. Kadjawaji. A piece of phosphorous spluttered in his guts. He realised that his hands were hard across Petronella's shoulders – tightening, fingers crushing. Holding her down, pushing her into the ground. He could feel the rise of her back as she fought for breath.

'Boysie?' Struggling to get words out. 'Why? Lynne? Why?'

He shushed her violently, hand in front of the shocked face, fingers outstretched motioning quiet. 'Your sister. Karen. On the wrong bloody side. Understand?'

Her face blank. No sign of comprehension.

'Lynne was. I thought Lynne was with me. Us. She thought I was. Klara. She thought. Oh Christ it's bloody difficult, darling. Just trust me, hu? Trust me. These people here are murder. I know.'

She was desperately frightened, shoulders quivering under his hands. Somehow her fear helped to repress the stark howl of terror ripping him apart. There were voices coming from along the shore. Agitated.

Calling. The sound of feet.

'Keep your head down and keep quiet.' His main instinct was to hide from his own shadow. To go on living for as long as possible. Petronella nodded violently – a cowering serf. In the middle of the panic Boysie was momentarily aware of a rising sexual need. Conscious of the material under his fingers. One hand moved from the girl's shoulder and caressed her buttocks, gently soothing. Then, in a wild rush he felt a whole pile of physical desires and feelings – sex hunger, the pain in his shoulder, the scratch on his hand, thirst and certain knowledge that it was a long time since he had been to the lavatory.

There were two men and two girls. Running, slithering over the pebbles. Crunching heavily as they broke out on to the beach. Then, a shorter, halt step. Kadjawaji limping along in the rear. Boysie could hear the sharp little pants of breath, like a dog excited after running for a stick. One of the girls called something, revulsion, distaste in her voice. They must have reached the shattered boat. Kadjawaji replied – a squeaky, piping note edged with authority.

Boysie swore as loudly as he dared. 'My gun. I've left me bleeding gun in the boat.'

Gingerly he raised himself on to one knee. Kadjawaji had joined the group who were trying to disentangle the thing that had once been Lynne from the smashed and scattered speedboat.

His concentration kept fluttering from idea to idea, like a crazed butterfly unable to settle. Lynne had said a path led to the villa's boathouse. The one down which Kadjawaji had just come? It could not be far. A hundred yards at the most. Amber Nine? What the hell was Amber Nine? And 'the fun'? Lynne had said that Kadjawaji had arrived 'just in time for the fun'. The boathouse. Make for the boathouse and then, maybe, back across the lake. He had a mental picture of himself in a skiff, rowing like the clappers. Speeded up. An old movie.

Boysie lowered his head and spoke softly. 'Trust me. I want you to move as quickly and as quietly as you can. To the left. There should be some kind of boat down there.'

They crawled forward, keeping in the undergrowth as far as possible. Exaggerating their steps, moving with unnatural caution. After a few yards the beach petered out replaced by reddish soil. The villa was directly ahead. A solidly built stone wall – the boathouse – with the strange distorted building on top. One door in the wall. Boysie turned the handle, and to his relief, the door swung inwards.

'Light switch?' He queried. They both felt along the wall. Petronella found it, low, near the door – a big fusebox handle. She pushed downwards as Boysie closed the door. A circle of Fresnel Spot lanterns, mounted on a wide central ring up near the roof, flashed on, accentuating the coldness of the air inside the building.

They were standing on a catwalk, water only a few inches from their toes. It was a vast pen with a narrow entrance – barred by a roll-up door – widening into a bay which comfortably held six heavy motor cruisers, each around eighteen feet overall, moored in two sets of three. Bolted to the bows of each craft a pair of Degtyarev light machine guns – stubby, obscene-looking silencers screwed to their snouts. The catwalk surrounded the whole bay. Water ski-ing equipment hung on the walls. But Boysie only took this in as part of the background. His eyes were fixed on the *piece de résistance*. Directly in front of them, filling the entire entrance bay, was a twenty-seven-foot craft. The bows and stern were those of a normal light vessel, but the sides bulged out like an elongated lift raft. Four troughs in the bows held four machine guns in a neat row forward of a streamlined cabin, large enough to hold at least a dozen people. After, a rear-facing triple-bladed airscrew and engine sprouted from a smooth aerofoil-shaped pedestal. Behind this, a high fin. The whole, like the motor cruisers, was painted in a sinister matt black.

'Oh, my gawd, a bloody great hovercraft.' Boysie could have cried. If Kadjawaji's lot were Klara's opposition it put Boysie firmly and unflinchingly on Klara's side of the railings. He was not sure of the unflinching bit, but obviously he had to get back to the island. Or at least to the other side of the lake. The only way across from the boathouse was on the hovercraft and he would really rather not try that. He opened the door a fraction. Then closed it, very fast, slamming the bolt into place. Kadjawaji was coming down the path with the two girls – all three armed, carefully searching the scrub and undergrowth. Boysie looked left, looked right, and then looked left again. There was a large door at the far end of the boathouse – obviously leading to the villa.

'They're coming this way. That door. Quick.' And he was off up the catwalk –

playing hare to Petronella's tortoise – his bare feet flip-flapping on the wet stones. Again a picture of the school swimming bath floated into his head.

The door was a recent addition to the building: steel, and locked from the outside. It would not take long for Kadjawaji to figure out their possible location. Boysie said *that* word. In this context it had nothing to do with sex. Back down the catwalk to the main roll-up garage-type door. Petronella plodding behind. On the wall another large switch was marked *Porta. Aperto. Chiuso.* The lever was in the *Chiuso* position. Electrically operated door. That was all right. Petronella stood on the catwalk looking lost and vacant.

'Please, Boysie, what's happening?'

'We're bloody trapped that's what's happening and if that short-arsed little curry-eater gets his hands on me – oh grief...' Boysie had a vivid vision of what would happen if Kadjawaji got him. 'We're going out.'

'In that?' A hand towards the hovercraft.

'If she's tanked up.'

'But do you know how to...?'

'Shouldn't be difficult.' Boysie's knees clipping against each other with a tympanic

240

resonance. After all he had once flown an aeroplane. Bile rushed into his mouth at the thought. It was not at all bad. Was it bloody hell? A shout from outside. One of the girls calling. Lord knew how many of Kadjawaji's mixed thugs were in the villa on the other side of the steel door.

'Up into the fiendish thing then.' He patted Petronella's bottom, trying to sound breezy, pushing her towards the thin metal ladder curving up the side of the craft. The cockpit, for two, was infernally like that of an aeroplane – rudder pedals, control column and half-wheel in front of the left-hand seat; two separate throttles and a bank of switches to the right. In front, a dashboard straight out of science fiction. There was a feeling of newness in the smell, the upholstery, even the way the hatch slid open.

'Ah yes,' said Boysie settling in the pilot's seat and tentatively touching the controls. His eyes did a swivel search for an instruction manual.

'Do you know *anything* about hovercraft?' Petronella dubious.

'Certain amount.' This consisted of a quick flip through an article in one of the Sundays. Boysie had retained little. There was something about plenum chambers and compressor fans, he remembered. Aloud he said, 'Hump speed and ram effect.' The *double entendre* of the two terms particularly fascinated him.

'Do what?'

'What? Oh yes, hump speed and ram effect. Not sure what they mean. Got something to do with drag – technically speaking, not kinky.'

'Boysie.'

'Hang on, let me figure this out.'

'But, do you think it's safe?'

'What?'

'Trying to drive this thing without...'

'Well it's not safe to stay here.'

'But...'

Boysie was getting touchy. It was bad enough having to work the machine. Now prattling women already. He got acid. 'Look, you can stay if you want to, but I'm for out. Right?'

'Right, Boysie.' Subservient.

Boysie relented a little. 'And while we're at it I feel terrible. I need mothering. A bloody great breast to cushion me cheek. I need loving. Right?'

'Right, Boysie, darling.' Leaning forward she kissed his cheek.

'I would not mind,' thought Boysie. 'Maybe she is a girls' girl, but I definitely would not mind.'

Pushing sex aside, he concentrated on the controls. Above the throttles two banks of switches stood in little erect rows; below them a pair of red buttons. *Compressor. Power.* Boysie argued that if he threw all the switches and pressed both buttons something ought to happen. His eyes ranged over the instrument panel, finally sorting out the fuel gauges. The needles were steady in the full position.

'We got sea lions in our tanks,' mused Boysie – the problems of galvanising the hovercraft into action temporarily erasing fear.

'From the top then. How long will it take you to get from the switchboard – the one by the doors – back into the cabin?'

'I haven't got to get out again?' Petronella on the brink of outrage.

'Yes.'

'But can't you do it?'

'Because I'll be wrestling with the controls, you lovely twit. As soon as that door begins to move I've got to get the engines turning.'

'All right.' Grudgingly. 'From the switch

back to the cabin? A minute at the most.'

Boysie checked that the door on his side was firmly closed, then leaned over and slid Petronella's hatch open to full – a tentative hint. 'Make it half a minute. Untie her first, she's moored fore and aft on your side. Then switch the doors to open and split-arse back – I mean get back here as quickly as you can.' He patted her shoulder, a stupid grin hiding the flesh-quake lying under the skin. 'Off you go. Good luck.'

'I love you, too.' A grimace. 'Don't go away.' She was out of the cabin, coming into view a few seconds later by the switch. Thumbs up. Thumbs up from Petronella. Switch down. The roll-up door began to lift – a shaft of natural light stripping into the boathouse. Petronella running back out of his line of vision.

Boysie made a dive for the switches on the dash, clicking them on – in threes – with the flat of his hand. An almighty whine swept upwards, and, as the last switches went on, so Boysie pressed the starter buttons. He could feel the power from behind. Glancing back through the glass of the cabin roof he saw the airscrew turning. A rumble from the bows – compressor fans starting to build up the lifting pressure of air around the craft.

The roll-up was fully open – a high oblong, cinemascope and 3D of the lake. Petronella clambered into the cabin, sliding her door. Boysie's hands moved the throttles forward, the roar and rumble rising. Louder.

'I wonder how the hell you get the thing moving?' He shouted easing back on the control column. 'They only fly about a foot high.' Comforting himself. 'I think.' Now they *were* moving. Backwards. A shudder and tearing noise as their stern hit the motor cruisers behind them – a poing-de-clank-poing sound usually associated with shunting yards – Boysie thrown forward, pushing on the control column. The hovercraft seemed to do a tango step to left, then right, hitting and bumping against the sides of the boathouse. Boysie piled on a bit of power. Unsteady, but fast, the craft wobbled out on to the lake.

'Hey, it works. You push forward to go forward.'

'They're on top of the boathouse.' Petronella twisted in her seat, craning to look back through the cabin. 'On the terrace. Oh god, they're shooting. Look out.'

There was a dull thump behind the growl of motors. Something shattering. Boysie's head whipped to one side. Part of the cabin roof was cracked into a cobweb where a bullet had struck.

'How the hell d'you steer this thing?' They seemed to be moving fast, steady and true, but Boysie had more than a vague suspicion that the slightest buffet would send them out of control. He pressed heavily on one of the rudder pedals. The world began to turn.

'Hang on,' yelled Boysie as they slewed about in a great circle, the craft almost turning on its own axis. He had never been particularly happy about the Big Dipper or the Waltzer since six of chips did a rebound from his stomach at the September Fair when he was ten years old. On that occasion he had ridden on both Waltzer and Dipper. Now, the sensation came back over the years with an appalling accuracy of taste, smell and general feeling. Petronella grabbed at the D-shaped safety handle in front of her seat. It pulled away slightly as she caught hold – puffs of smoke appearing forward of the cabin. Boysie felt the recoil. PS-type 7.62 mm bullets (with the mild steel core) pumping out of the Degtyarevs at the rate of 650 a minute. The beach and villa were sliding through Boysie's sight-line. Bullet splashes on the water. Stonework chipping. People ducking for cover on the terrace.

Down near the boathouse doors Kadjawaji trying to disguise himself as a pile of pebbles.

'Let go of that. It's the trigger. The guns. For Pete's sake you'll kill someone.'

Petronella let go and the spurt of bullets from the bows stopped. Boysie had got his foot off the rudder pedals and they were moving parallel to the shore. Perilously close. Getting closer.

'Shook 'em up a bit.' Petronella, pleased.

'Probably shook one or two early risers as well. Wish I could point this bloody boat in the right direction.' Boysie gave the left rudder pedal gentle pressure. Very careful. Edgy, in case they started doing sharp turns again. The bows moved a fraction to the left. He had some control now. Experimenting again he applied more pressure. The bows slid round. In the far distance the Brissago islands were clearly visible. Tender pressure until the bows lined up with islands. On course. No *erratic* movements. He must remember. Daringly, Boysie tried the control wheel. They bucketed like a banking aeroplane, churning up a mist of spray. A plunge in the lower bowel. No more experiments. Just keep the thing straight and level, bounding over the water.

'They're trying to get one of the motor boats out.' Petronella giving a running commentary, leaning back to get a better view of the shore. 'No, it's all right. The little man is calling them back. They're not following.'

'Too fast for 'em.' Boysie grinned and inched the throttles forward. 'Simple once you know.' The craft wallowed for a second, swung to the right and pitched slightly. When things were under control again he had another go at the grin. 'See?'

'My hero,' said Petronella with a tincture of acid. She allowed a small smile to filter over her lips, dropped her head in a spur-of-the-moment gesture pressing it against Boysie's shoulder. 'No, you've been wonderful.' Straightening up. 'Boysie Oakes, the man with the built-in luck.'

'That's it. It's always luck. I never seem to accomplish anything through my consummate skill. Reckon I must have nine lives.' The grin turned to a look of nausea.

'You? You'll live to be a hundred and get a telegram.'

'Don't want a rotten telegram. I'd rather have the rotten money.'

'Oh, Boysie, love. For you I might change the hormones of a lifetime.' She laughed, the hint of a secret joke.

Boysie remembered the BOAC advertisement he had seen in the paper on the way over – *There's Always Time for a New Experience.* He was not thinking in terms of riding on a cushion of air, across the flat surface of Maggiore at – what was it? The airspeed indicator read thirty-five knots but that meant little because he could not remember how to convert knots into miles. Or was it the other way round?

'Boysie?'

Her glanced at her – the craft dipping slightly as concentration wavered. There were dark smudge marks of fatigue under her eyes and the face looked thinner than it had been over the lunch table at the *Palmira* yesterday. Less than twenty-four hours ago.

'Yes?'

'I've trusted you. I could have gone for you back there in the boat, in the speedboat. Saved Lynne.' A sharp cough, an emotional tickle in the throat.

'What stopped you?'

'The name. What was it? Khavisomething?'

'Khavichev. Big man. Chief of their Counterespionage. Equivalent of our Paymaster-General or the Director of the CIA.'

'Thought he didn't come from a good

Anglo-Saxon family. Tell me about it? I mean is Klara not…?'

'Don't really know. Nothing makes sense – except the obvious. Lynne's people are Khavichev's people which makes Klara the lesser of the two evils. She must be OK – I've just remembered, she used our code for radio silence. She said "incommunicado". Lousy for you. Your Karen on the other side.'

A deep V creased between her eyebrows.

'It'll ruin my father.'

'There'll be screenings and questions.' Boysie knew well enough how they would take Wing Commander Whitching through the mill. And his family. The smooth quiet gentleman he had often met in Mostyn's office. The boys in the velvet-collared overcoats. All dressed by *The Tailor and Cutter.* University men down to the balls of their hard little feet. Putting you at ease then stripping your mind with the efficiency of a shoal of piranha going over a cadaver. Petronella's professional father would have little career left when they had finished with him. Brainy all of them. Too brainy if you were innocent.

'Have we got to go back to her.'

Boysie was still thinking of the interrogators. The searchers.

'Boysie?'

'What? Sorry.'

'Do we have to go back to the island? To Klara Thirel?'

'I do. She's got to be told about Ingrid for a start. Drop you off first if you like.'

They covered another hundred yards.

'No, I'd like to get at the truth.'

Boysie nodded. 'Whatever?'

'Whatever.'

They were within half-a-mile of the islands. From this side the house loomed large and grey behind a palisade of trees. In the foreground a small wall held back the lake. There was a dinghy moored near by, and a stone slipway which looked wide enough to take the hovercraft. It all romped closer every second. Boysie started to ease back on the throttles, cutting down speed. Soon he would have to face stopping the wretched machine.

'They go on land as well as water, don't they?' he shouted, doubt tangling with his vocal chords.

'I think so.' Petronella anticipated the problem. 'Why don't you stop now and let us drift in?'

'It'll look bloody silly. Rather try and give the impression of expertise. Arrive in a blaze of glory.'

'Or gasoline.' Petronella looked round for something to grab when the time came. Her hand fluttered on the guns' trigger.

'And don't touch that for Chrissake.'

The slipway was getting very close. Boysie reduced power. As low as he dared, bringing the airspeed indicator needle a paper-width from the red line which he presumed was the stalling speed. Yet they were still moving with considerable momentum. It was like putting on ineffective brakes. What if they did not slide neatly up the ramp? It would be quite a bump. There was some activity on the island, figures moving along the wall. Concentrate. The slipway appeared to rise out of the water at a ridiculous angle. Fifty feet. Power reduced a fraction more. Juddering. Without noticeable slackening of speed. Forty feet. Thirty. Twenty. They were going to smash straight into it. Still going too fast. Ten feet. Petronella screamed. Boysie lost his nerve and cut back on both throttles. The craft began to move effortlessly up the ramp. Then it hovered, buffeting as though it would fall apart. A series of red lights flickered on from the dashboard, and they dropped with a slushy sound. Not the bang but the whimper. They were at a standstill, half in and half out of the water, poised on the slipway. Boysie slid his hatch open, leaned out and took a lungful of air.

'Come on Pet, I'll help you down.'

They had to climb into a good four feet of water. At the top of the slipway stood the two blond gentlemen with whom Boysie had crossed swords at the *Madonna Del Sasso*. Neither looked happy at the reunion. Both wore similar blue denim suits. One had a bandaged head, the other a plaster cast on his right arm. The swordsticks were not in evidence. Instead they held Mauser automatics. They advanced down the slipway towards Boysie and Petronella, a single intention in their eyes.

'Now look, fellows,' said Boysie, pushing an invisible wall away from him with the flat of his hands as he came up from the lake. 'Look...' He stumped and slid back into the water, getting a mouthful. He spat and gave a tired sigh. 'Aw heck. Look, take me to your leader, hu?'

CHAPTER ELEVEN

TANGERINE WHATSITS:
ISOLE DI BRISSAGO

Large pips of pain bombarded Martin's right knee cap. He tried to be fatalistic about it. After all, one could not deny the power of that kneecap. It had yet to be proved wrong. Just like his mother, he thought. Only she told you when it was going to rain. Rheumatic twinges in the left elbow she got. Infallible. But this was not merely a case of rain. Rarely had the knee been so bad. This would be the full *donner und blitz*. The *1812* with the guns and bells. The real *Strudel*.

There had been delays all the way. First, the wait at London Airport, then a further hanging around in Zürich. It was nine-thirty in the morning before Martin finally walked into the elaborate foyer of the *Palmira* – a little plush for Martin's bed-sitterish tastes. He sighed the registration form with a nervous flourish.

254

'Ah. Mr Martin.' The gangling concierge discreetly peeped at the signature. 'There is a cable for you.'

Until then the pain had just niggled. This was the moment of its full flowering.

The cable said:

HEAD OFFICE SUGGEST I JOIN YOU STOP HAVE ARRANGED HEL FLIGHT SPECIAL CHA 14 ARRIVING MONTE CENERI NOON STOP REQUEST MEET ME PREFERABLY WITH OUR LIQUID SAMPLE STOP UNCLE STOP.

Mostyn was on his way. Martin had to meet him at the airport with Boysie. He crumpled the telegram into his pocket. The sober, dark blue Galashiels Homespun felt conspicuous, out of place with the spring sun beaming down like a mad thing.

'Room 234, Mr Martin. The boy will look after your baggage. We hope you have a good stay.'

'I believe there's a friend of mine staying here.'

'Sir?' pleased and helpful, the concierge was the Swiss ideal – gleaming quiet comfort and service, from the polished shoes to the shining crossed keys on his lapels.

'Mr Oakes. Brian Oakes. Brian Ian Oakes.'

The concierge's face underwent a mild, just detectable, change. Normally it would have gone unnoticed, but Martin – formerly a trained, though dull, journalist – was quick with these things.

'There's something wrong?'

'Oh no, sir.' Very quick. 'Mr Oakes is a guest in the hotel.'

'His room number?' Eyebrows raised questioningly.

Embarrassment. 'Room 472. But you will not find him there, Mr Martin. He has gone out.'

'Out?'

'Out.'

'You expect him back?'

The concierge spread his hands wide. Then, confidentially: 'You are a close friend?'

Martin did his famous omnipotent move – eighty per cent smile, twenty per cent laugh. It suggested that he knew everything, from all angles. 'As close as a brother.'

Boysie had been out on the previous afternoon, Martin had learned that in Mostyn's office. He was worried.

'When did he leave?'

'That is the point, sir. He left yesterday afternoon.'

Another flair of pain.

'Well?'

'Well, sir.'The concierge, doing an inverted version of Martin's move – eighty per cent laugh and twenty per cent smile.

'There was a young woman.' As if that explained the whole *kibbutz*.

'Do I know her?'

The concierge shrugged and remained silent.

'Try me.'

'It was a Miss Whitching.' He pronounced it Wee Ching. Could have been Chinese. 'Miss Petronella Whitching.' Accenting the 'on' in Petronella. 'She is also a guest and...'

'She has not returned either.'

The concierge nodded. Big knowing nods.

Martin wagged his head in irritated understanding.

'It's important that I find him quickly.' He gave the impression of a reward. 'We work for the same firm. Did he call anyone yester-day?'

'I don't think... Yes. Yes, sir, he did. He called the *Muralo* – the little hotel down the road.'

Martin had seen the *Muralo* on his way from the station. It was nearly as big as the *Palmira*.

'Anyone in particular, or just a friendly word to all the guests?'

'Ha-ha. Hu.' Such a good sense of humour the English. 'I am trying to remember. I put the call through for him. It was to a Mr Gold … Gold…'

'Finger?' said Martin with some alarm.

'No-no-no.' Searching the memory. 'Gold … blat. Mr Goldblat.'

'Would you like to get him for me? On the telephone.'

'I'll have it put through to your room, sir.'

Martin smiled affably. 'See you later then.'

'Not me, sir. I have a two-day holiday now. For the week-end I go away.'

Martin fumbled for his folding francs.

'Mr Goldblat?' Martin's call came through within seconds of the door closing behind the departing bellboy.

'Goldblat 'ere. That you agin, Mr Oakes?'

The voice, Martin thought, identified Goldblat as one of proletarian origin.

'No actually it isn't. I wondered if he was with you.'

'What? Oakes?' Wary.

'Yes.'

'E's not with me, chum. No. You a friend of 'is then?'

'A friend, yes. A friend and colleague. We

258

work for the same firm.'

'Ah, well I can't help you Mr ... er...?'

'Martin. You know Oakes well?'

'No, not really. Acquaintance like. Sorry I can't 'elp, Mr Martin.'

Martin could almost see the receiver poised over the rests. 'Look, Mr Goldblat, don't hang up. This is rather important. You've no idea where he's gone? Seems to have disappeared.'

At the other end, Griffin tried to hedge. He liked Oakes. 'Tell yer what. 'E was out with a bird yesterday.'

'I know that.'

'Ah. Then 'e was going off to some snobby birds' finishin' school.'

'You sure?'

'Yes. Picked up with 'im on the train comin' down 'ere. We was goin' out for a bit of a booze last night, then 'e rung me and said as 'ow 'e 'ad to go off to this birds' finishing place. For smart birds it was,' lied Griffin, with a gloss finish.

Martin was stuck. 'You staying on long, Mr Goldblat. I'd like to have a talk.'

'Couple of days.'

'I'll be in touch. If that's all right?'

'Yer. Yer. You do that.'

Martin burbled his thanks and put down

the telephone. Up the road at the *Muralo* Griffin thought it was about time to do something – like getting back to London, or something.

Mostyn was in an ugly mood. He kept offering snide advice to Martin who was at the wheel of the Rent-A-Car Merc 230SL.

'Just watch it, old Martin. Don't want you to be involved in a road incident do we?'

'No, sir.' He was still getting the feel of the car – and of driving on what, to him, would always be the wrong side of the road.

'Grief,' said Mostyn with over emphasis as they shaved a cyclist – a girl, trying to manage the bicycle with one hand and her skirt with the other. 'She'd've looked nice sprayed silver on the bonnet.'

Martin negotiated a long bend around which two motor coaches seemed to be doing a ton. When they reached a straight stretch, coming into the outskirts of Locarno, Mostyn got back to the matter in hand.

'You didn't visit this Goldblat?'

'Didn't have time. What with being late, and your cable, and hiring the car. It's a long drive out to Monte Ceneri. We can stop in at the *Muralo* on our way to Brissago if you like.'

Mostyn looked at his watch. 'No time now. Better get straight out there and see what's cooking.'

They plunged into the more dense traffic crawling through Locarno. Mostyn changed his tactics.

'The old firm, eh?'

'I beg your pardon, sir.'

'The old firm. Mostyn and Martin.'

'Oh yes, sir.' Without thinking, 'And Boysie.'

'Yes.' Mostyn's face hardened to the texture of flint. 'Yes, and Boysie.' The vocal pitch would have satisfied any devotee of the Theatre of Cruelty. 'Bloody Boysie Oakes.'

They were passing the bus station and depot for the Centovalli Railway – the long blue and white coaches bearing, on each side, the initials FART.

'B... O...' said Mostyn.

'B... O...' Breathed Boysie in a hollow whisper, like the television ad. He was lying on his back examining the lighter which, with his cigarettes, had been returned to him. Under the circumstances Klara had shown a great deal of restraint. Cool, but ready to listen. After she had heard Boysie's side of the story she picked up the telephone.

'Angela? Where's Ingrid?'

Boysie could hear the yackity noise of the female voice at the other end, floating across the desk from the earpiece.

'Good. Take two of the girls and put her under close arrest. Be careful. She may be armed; she may resist. Treat her as an enemy.'

Surprise sounds from Angela.

'Now. This instant. Just do as I say, then take her along to number four cubical and wait until I send for you.'

She looked over the desk at Boysie, whose attention was distracted for a moment by Hector banging his revolting hairy front legs against the glass door of his home. Though the nest was a good six feet away, Boysie cringed. The legs made a phdump-dump sound on the glass. Klara smiled.

'That does not mean I am convinced, but I have to play it safe. You understand, Boysie?'

Boysie wagged his head – enthusiastically, like a pleased puppy.

'You will be looked after with care and consideration but, I'm afraid, under maximum security. Now I will talk with the unfortunate Miss Whitching.'

The two blond men – who were called

Cyril and Frederick – took him off through the underlake maze, stood over him while he bathed, shaved (gear provided by *Il Portone*) and dressed. His own clothes – the ones he had been wearing before the *Madonna Del Sasso* incident – were waiting for him: cleaned, pressed and with the small rent, made by Cyril's sword blade, invisibly mended. Back along the corridors to the cells.

'Doctor Thirel said to give you these,' lisped Frederick. With all that talent around it was not surprising that Klara's strong arm couple were screaming queers. He took the offered cigarettes, watch and lighter, and walked into the cell. Ten minutes later Angela came in bearing a tray – coffee, eggs, bacon, toast and Keiller's Dundee marmalade. The girl looked flushed and worried.

Smiling half-heartedly, she put down the tray. 'A real English breakfast.'

'No kidneys in a silver dish and people in white trousers sauntering in saying "Anyone for tennis?" Don't think I'll bother,' said Boysie briskly.

Angela managed a laugh.

'Stay and keep me company.' Boysie patted the bed on which he was lying.

'Some other time.' She was off through the

door. Two other Seniors hovered outside. One carried a sub-machine gun. Klara was not going to take any chances this time. Boysie looked at his breakfast and the gastric juices bubbled. An hour later he was replete and asleep.

His watch showed five minutes past one when he woke, but it was impossible to tell whether it was afternoon, or if he had slept right through the day and into the next. Boysie lit a cigarette, coughed a little, stretched back on the bed and examined the lighter.

'B... O...' He breathed. Should really have had his full initials engraved on the *Windmaster*. Just BO was not really his right style. It left him open to rude and vulgar comment. BIO – for Brian Ian Oakes – would have been better. Years ago, at school, he had BIO over everything. Even looked it up in the dictionary and commited it to memory – it seemed to suit him: Bio – *prefix*. (Course of) life of, concerning, organic life.' Boysie's mind, being what it was, the word 'organic' took him straight on to 'orgasm'. Hands shaking. Ageless instincts. He sighed. It was not that he was promiscuous. Mentally he was not promiscuous. He just needed a lot of love – especially when under strain. The absurd life into which he had stumbled made it absolutely necessary. A woman one liked, even loved a little; who would react like a dancing partner; there had to be give and take; it had to be mutual in order to make that cocoon of warmth, safety, contact and pleasure. The way Mostyn talked about it you would think the whole business was dirty. It was obvious what kind of man Mostyn was. Like a bull. 'Wham-wham thank you ma'am,' and away. A taker. Nothing of a giver about Mostyn. Boysie's body was disturbed.

As if in answer to a prayer the key turned and Angela ushered Petronella into the cell.

'Thought you'd like some company, Mr Oakes.' She was out again quickly, the door shut and the key turned. Petronella leaned against the wall smiling at him.

'Hey,' said Boysie swivelling into a sitting position – all his sexual self-appraisal crumbling into lechery. Petronella was wearing a washed out denim skirt with low pleats, and a silk shirt which looked as though it had come from a Dior Boutique for Men. Her hair was brushed back from the forehead clear away from the deep hazel eyes glittering with the look of one well rested. The skirt was too small – as much as two inches short and hugging the hips fetchingly.

'You like it?'

'I was just thinking...' His voice trailed off, remembering that he had shared this very bed with Petronella on the night before. A far from memorable episode.

'So was I, Boysie. That's why I asked Angela to bring me down – she lent me the gear by the way.'

Boysie went on goggling.

'I've an apology to make.'

'Hu-hu.'

'I lied to you last night.'

'Woman thy name is frailty,' he misquoted.

'I know. Things are not always what they seem. Some girls wear fake engagement rings – wedding rings even. I pull the Lesbian stunt.'

'Full of deceit.'

'Chock full.' A slight rise of the colour. Stage one of a blush. 'I can't unless I have some real feelings, and last night you made it quite obvious that you didn't...'

'Ah.' Then, hurriedly. 'Well, you see, last night I...'

'No need to explain.' The woman scorned. 'I just wanted to let you know that I was sorry. Sorry I lied.'

'Well, that was yesterday.'

'Yes.'

'It's a new day. Or is it?'

'Day.'

'Good. Let's make a new start. The brave new world. Walking hand in hand towards the horizon and a fresh beginning. Fade out to a splurge of music and we all jam the exits trying to get out before they play the National Anthem.'

'Rectify things?'

'Why not.'

'You bronzed monster you.' Pleased. Petronella's hand came out of her skirt pocket. She was holding a small square of sticking plaster. 'Angela again,' she said, fixing the plaster over the door's peep hole.

'That girl thinks of everything.

Petronella turned and unzipped the skirt. 'That's a relief, it was cutting me in two.' There was no restraint.

'Rending you in twain,' said Boysie giving his eyes a six-course banquet. The shirt came off in one. The Mary Quants were gone – their places taken by cheeky little nylon bra and pants; frilled, warm orange.

'I say. Tangerine whatsits. Angela's!'

'She was glad to get rid of them. They're not regulation here and Klara's about to have a pantie purge.' She was advancing toward the bed, arms doubled behind her, dealing with the brassière. It fell away. Boysie's head whizzed as he pulled her on to the bed beside him. An arm streaked up his spine to the short hairs on the back of his neck. Mouths met in a skirmish which developed into a pitched battle of lips, teeth and tongues. Fingers traced up his thighs, caught his hand and tried to lift it to the deep valley between her breasts, but Boysie disengaged, running his nails gently across the lower part of her chest, over the well of her navel, and down the quivering stomach. Cupping his fingers he closed around the thin nylon and began to draw gently downwards. Petronella moaned – not anguish or pain but the throaty call of the female in need. A shifting. Movement. The hard unmistakable thrill. Another rocking moan. Movement.

Bingo. It was like an enquiry agent's flashlight exploding in a seedy hotel bedroom. The key clanked suddenly and the door swung open.

'BoySIE!' said Mostyn, the last syllable reaching a shattering roar. Behind him stood Martin and two of the girls.

Desire deflated. 'You would,' said Boysie through teeth grinding more than clenching. 'You bloody would. You send me out on your do or bloody die assignments... You... You got me mixed up in all kinds of subversive goings on, then bloody walk in on me just as I'm going to score. You Sh...'

'OAKES!'

Boysie knew the tone. There was no arguing with it. Mostyn like that? You listen.

Mostyn at least had the courtesy to turn his back while Petronella dressed. He did, however, talk – at speed and not in Boysie's favour.

'Only you, Oakes. Nobody but you, Oakes, could possibly reach such revolting depths of lunacy. You unmitigated bloody purblind idiot. As a member of the department you'd make a good assistant to a pox doctor's clerk. Not only do you get yourself put down by our own people...'

'How the hell was I to know they were our own people.'

'Initiative, old Oakes. Your half-witted quarter-formed, stinking rotten initiative.'

'Look, it's their fault. They jumped me. How was I to know.'

'I've heard all about that. Klara Thirel's been running this establishment in our favour for eight years, and in twenty-four hours you ram everything up the spout.'

'I'm asking you. How was I to know?'

'You should have made deductions.'

'You didn't tell me. In the briefing you didn't tell me.'

'I didn't know.'

'Well then.'

'Well nothing. You should have worked it out for yourself. You're the one in the field.'

'Rot the rotting rotten field.'

'I've cleared you with Doctor Thirel anyway. She's interrogating the girl – Ingrid. I think we'd better go up.'

'Look, sir. What's it all about? Please?'

Mostyn tapped his foot in agitation. 'That girl got her knickers on yet?'

'Yes. And my skirt and shirt. Gentlemen should always knock before...' Petronella looked as though steam was about to come out of her ears. Mostyn signalled to the two Seniors.

'Take her up to the villa and wait there. Don't let her out of your sight.'

Boysie tried to smile at the departing Petronella, but she did not even glance in his direction. She left with head down, the twin spots of fury and humiliation burning bright on her cheeks. Mostyn came into the room, banging the door in Martin's face.

'Women, Oakes, are your bloody downfall.

With women you're a psychopath. You never learn. There have been times, old Oaksie, that you have put the Department – nay, the world...' He liked the ring of that. 'Nay, the world – in danger because of women.' His voice had modulated to the sharpness of a cut-throat razor just touching the windpipe. 'Remember Miss Iris bloody MacIntosh? Coral White strike a cord? Or Priscilla Whatsername...?'

'Braddock-Fairchild.'

'Yes. And that American one, Lettuce Triplearse.'

'Chicory Triplehouse,' said Boysie, venomous.

'And hundreds more. I've no doubt at all. Hundreds more. I warned you about this before we took you on.'

'Conned me into it.'

'I came out here all the way from London, to get you out of the jam you've got yourself into and what do I find?'

'We've become very close friends. We've been through a great deal together, Petronella and I, me, I.'

'I'll say, old Boysie. It looked like it. Now I've really got something on you, laddie. I wish I'd had my Polaroid with me.'

'Colonel? Please tell me what's happening.'

The storm had blown out. Mostyn filled his lungs and licked his thin little lips. 'Briefly. Ten years ago Klara Thirel made a third-party approach to Security. It was the off season – most of the top brass on holiday. The man who finally saw her thought she was a nut and passed the buck to the Chief of Training Command – on the old-boy basis of course. He met her and saw the potential. Checked. Double-checked. Sent someone over here as a prospective parent to give the school the once-over, then put a couple of our girls in for a year. Everything came up roses. Financially marvellous. Klara Thirel, believe it or not, can train agents for fifty per cent of what it costs us. He made a deal. Natch.' Mostyn paused to extract a pig-skin cigarette case from the inside of his jacket. Boysie refused the proffered *Passing Cloud*. Mostyn lit, drew heavily and continued.

'Gets girls from all over. Screening system's better than ours. Some just our type. She selects them, weeds 'em out and trains 'em. The school's genuine enough, and the whole set-up allows specialised training without disrupting the normal curriculum.' He stabbed a forefinger down at the floor – a series of jabbing movements, like an orator accentuating a point of argument. 'For eight years Training Comand've been filling female vacancies *in all Deparrments* with girls from *Il Portone*. That means about twelve first-class operatives a year. It's cheaper, and Training Command hasn't told a living soul.'

'They wouldn't, would they? I mean Klara's dad wasn't exactly pro-British. And they're operating in a neutral country. Sticky.'

'As a baby's top lip. Very high risk-ratio. I mean, Old Boysie, we've been taking a chance on you – and your successor; the old "kill assignments". But they're only domestic next to this. Training Command are inviting global difficulties. World opinion wouldn't take kindly. Could be an embarrassment.'

'Who's going to be the next Chief of Training Command?' Fiendish relish.

'Precisely.' Mostyn sniggered – a jackal peeping from its lair. Mostyn had long lusted after a Department of his own.

'And the *au pair* thing? Kadjawaji?'

'Part of the embarrassment. The opposition's known about the school for a long while. They've been putting their own girls in with monotonous regularity, as you know. Mostly the *au pair* lot, who seem to have been recruited on the continent, dispersed

273

in England for brief training before being sent here. A bit amateur and it hasn't paid off. The only successful infiltration is the wretched Ingrid girl, and I suspect she's semi-professional. Never works, old boy. Never use amateurs.'

'I never get the chance. What's the object anyway?'

'Harassing operation, I presume. Disruption of the school leading to us breaking our contract with Dr Thirel. Maybe bigger. Public European scandal perhaps – and we can't afford that.'

'And Kadjawaji?'

Mostyn opened the door. Martin stood outside looking placid.

'What the hell are you doing there?'

'W-Waiting for you, sir.'

'Oh.' He turned to Boysie again. 'Kadjawaji? That's what we're hoping to find out from the Ingrid person. Doctor Thirel said you mentioned Assault One.'

'They're on the other side of the lake. Kadjawaji very much in charge.'

'Pinched a hovercraft, I hear.'

'The only thing to do.'

'Good lad. Assault One is a subversive security group. Sort of counter-espionage commando. Opposition's already used them

274

in the satellite countries. And Cuba – in the early days.'

'Tough?'

'Very. Both sexes. Sympathetic mercenaries mostly. Malcontents, failed belligerent CND people from all nations. Military trained as well as security. They can do most things – from jumping out of aeroplanes to organising unrest.'

'And here?'

'Straightforward violence I should imagine. Damage beyond repair made to look like an accident. Stop our flow of female operatives for a while.'

'Pow. Goodbye, Klara.'

'Farewell *Il Portone*. Northing we could do about it. Except reorganise our women's training programme. And the facilities of course. Now if I was in charge, old Boysie, I think I would…' He stopped in mid dream. 'Let's see what the intriguing Ingrid's got to say for herself.'

'Before we go, sir.' Boysie like an anxious schoolboy soliciting a favourite master. 'What about Amber Nine?'

Mostyn turned and looked at him with pity. 'That, my dear old Boysie, is our largest headache.'

'Largest.'

'Biggest. No aspirin will aid us. Four, five, six degrees under. Just cool nerves, dry powder and bowels open. Time enough.' He turned to Martin who had been trying to look inconspicuous. 'Just keep old Boysie in the picture will you? Your newspaper cutting.'

Martin began searching his person, finally finding a crumpled sheet of newspaper which he handed over.

'Might interest you. Net closing in and all that,' said Mostyn.

It was the front page of the *Evening Standard*. Late final edition. Yesterday's date.

'Down there,' Martin pointed to a heading at the bottom of columns three and four. Boysie read:

DOUBLE ARREST IN WIMBLEDON

Official Secrets Charges

Officers of Scotland Yard's Special Branch swooped on a quiet Wimbledon villa this afternoon and made two arrests.

Robert Wilson Wheater – described as a retired colonel – and Maude Bernice Wheater, both of 'Dunroamin', Ash Close,

Wibledon, were charged under the Official Secrets Act and later taken to London.

A police spokesman said it was not in the public interest to elaborate on the charges at this time.

The arrests were made just before two o'clock this afternoon when three cars pulled into select Ash Close. Detectives walked up the flagged path, through the trim little garden, bright with coloured stone gnomes, and knocked at the duck-egg blue door.

Tonight, the house was still being searched. Officers have already taken away several large boxes and packages.

A neighbour said: 'It is all very distressing. Two local councillors live in the Close. Colonel and Mrs Wheater have been here for five years and seemed perfectly respectable. Nothing like it has happened before. Now, I suppose, some of the residents will move. The tone has been lowered.'

'Come on, Boysie, get your skates on.' Mostyn was already striding up the passage. 'Wheater was Assault One's London control if it's any interest. And you wanted me to ring him. They're grilling him now.'

'Lynne's father?'

'Don't be naïve, childe Boysie. Shouldn't think he ever met the girl. Come on, let's see if Ingrid's squealing.'

She was. Loudly. Boysie heard her as they crossed the big gymnasium. A scream, followed by a shivering sob, coming from behind the doors leading into the fencing room, and eventually, to Klara's study. Mostyn pushed open the doors and Boysie recoiled at the bizarre sight. In the centre of the smaller gym stood an old-fashioned vaulting horse – a long leather sausage with four stubby wooden legs. Ingrid was spreadeagled and bent over the horse, her wrists and ankles shackled to the legs on either side. She was naked, her buttocks scarlet with two angry welts slicing across them, livid and raw. She sobbed horribly. Klara stood beside the horse, the riding crop in her right hand. The door to the study was open. Beside it, Angela and three of the Seniors lined the wall, rigidly at attention.

'Ready to tell us about your friends yet, Ingrid dear?' purred Klara.

The yellow fall of hair, on the far side of the horse, shook violently. Klara stepped back. The riding crop whistled viciously through the air and struck across the naked backside with a burning force. Ingrid screamed again.

Boysie muttered angrily, starting forward. Mostyn put out a hand and caught his arm. The Second-in-Command was quietly shaking his head, restraining Boysie.

'Ah,' said Klara. 'Come in, gentlemen. I'm afraid our young woman has lost her tongue for the moment.' Ingrid's sobs had turned to a long shuddering moan. Klara joined the men at the door – as spry as ever, smiling and completely unperturbed.

'Boysie.' She put a hand out. 'How can I ever apologise? I'm so glad it's all been sorted out.'

Boysie stared at her, his face flabby, as though drunk, the facial nerves refusing to act. Klara turned to Mostyn, her smile still set in the charm position.

'As you see, Colonel, I don't believe in the subtle ways of extracting information. We want this quickly and I have no time for the finer points of interrogation – pep drugs and depressants, the techniques of brain washing, sodium pentathol. For this, pain is the most effective drug.' She swished the riding crop, making the air sing. Even the girls by the door winced. Ingrid screamed again.

'That's interesting,' said Mostyn with the

concern of a professional. 'You're getting a conditioned reflex.'

'She has had three strokes only. She might be stubborn, but she'll crack. I've never failed yet.' She flexed the arm again. 'Ready to chat, Ingrid?' Again the head shaking. 'Very well. Back to the treatment. Unless anyone has a better idea.' She looked questioningly towards Mostyn.

'Permission, Principal.' Angela took a step forward.

'Yes.'

Angela came over, bent slightly and whispered. Klara was serious for a moment, then her face split into a pleased smile.

'Yes. Yes. Very good indeed. Go ahead. Prepare her.'

Angela returned to the other girls, spoke to them briefly and went into Klara's office. The girls moved quickly – like a demonstration team from one of the Women's Services. One of the big fibre mats was pulled aside. In the floorboards beneath, Boysie could see four metal bolt holes set at equal distances, like the corners of a square. While one girl screwed large iron eyes into the holes, the other two began to unshackle Ingrid from the horse. By this time, Angela had returned with three cushions. Together, the girls lifted Ingrid from the horse – only a mild struggle from their captive – and placed her on her back between the metal eyes. Angela slipped a cushion under the scarred buttocks and the shackles were snapped around the eyes. Now, Ingrid was once more spreadeagled – this time, undignified, on her back in the middle of the floor, the remaining cushions pushed behind her head, as though to hold it up so that she could look down at her own body.

It was a very beautiful body, still twisted with pain and shaking with the uncontrolled whimpering which seemed to saturate every nerve. Long firm legs, tanned golden from the sun, turning to contrasting white at the extreme points of the thighs – the tan taken up again just below the navel and stopping around the small raised circlets of breast. Boysie had never really looked at her face. Normally it must have been handsome more than pretty. Now, drained white with fear and pain, blotched with puffy red around the streaming eyes, it was the face of a child struck by some terrible private grief. Boysie wanted to scream with her. His palms ran with sweat – the whole process of cruelty repellent to him. Angela had made a second trip into Klara's study, this time returning with a small box, instantly recognisable to Boysie whose bones seemed to transmogrify into blancmange (Caréme's recipe). He remembered Ingrid on the previous evening in Klara's study, pressed against the wall in terror.

'What are they up to?' whispered Mostyn.

'Cows,' muttered Boysie. 'Sadistic bloody Friesians.'

Klara stood over Ingrid, slowly opening the box.

'Ingrid. We want to hear about your friends in Assault One. We want to know their plans. How? When? Where?'

'Stuff it,' sniffed Ingrid with spirit.

'As you like. Perhaps you will talk for a little friend of yours.'

The girl's body stiffened. Klara dropped to one knee and placed something on the floor near Ingrid's foot. Then again, this time between the hillocks of her bare breasts. Ingrid was trying to move, swaying from side to side, tearing and pulling – the chains on her manacles rattling. Boysie knew the feeling, the first onslaught of real fear. He recognised the look in her eyes – wide, constantly moving, afraid of the blow but wanting to know when it would strike.

'All right,' called Klara.

Angela's voice – 'OK' – from the study. Then a scampering like a kitten.

'Naaaaaow.' Hysterical, from Ingrid, threshing about in profound mental agony.

'He won't hurt you, Ingrid. Not if you lie still.'

Boysie felt Mostyn move back towards the door as Hector came pattering in from the study. The spider looked even more revolting than when Boysie had last seen him – its great legs at full stretch, moving unerringly towards Ingrid's foot.

'Good boy,' said Klara, coaxing. 'Grasshoppers. That's it. One there and one higher up.' She did a little dance step towards the three men (Martin well to the rear looking unquestionably seedy).

'Wasn't Angela clever to remember? Ingrid has a phobia about spiders. Terrified.'

'Arachnophobia already,' said Mostyn with a brutal purse of the lips.

Boysie could not move – rooted by the aura of ultimate hysteria which surrounded the girl, and the tingling creep of his own loathing.

The beast had gobbled the grasshopper by Ingrid's foot. Now an exploratory leg moved round the girl's ankle. The two hairy feelers edged on to her calf. With a jump, Hector was up on her thigh, the legs bent, lifting the oval furry body high, swaying obscenely. Ingrid gave a massive shiver and then went rigid, shock temporarily locking every nerve and muscle. From her lips came a low wordless blubber, rising.

Slowly the spider's head moved from side to side, as if trying to scent the grasshopper still balanced between the girl's breasts. Hector moved higher, the crawling legs stroking for a hold on the smooth flesh inside Ingrid's thigh. High. Higher, and up until the whole black repulsive creature was silhouetted creeping against the unsunned skin of the girl's belly. Boysie's flesh crinkled with a million spiders. He could feel the chilling tickle of Hector's legs, the tight suction as they took hold, and the weight of his own body. It began to climb between Ingrid's breasts – a leg moving up the curve brushing a nipple.

'No.' Ingrid's voice breaking on the borderline of panic. 'No I'll tell you. Please. PLEase. PLEASE.' A scream flaking the air, needling into the eardrums. 'I'll tell you.' Each word screeched into inaudibility. 'Get him away. Get him off. Away. I'll tell you... Everything. Anything. Away.'

Boysie could not stay to see or hear more. He turned and stumbled out into the large gymnasium. Hanging on to the wall bars. Count. Must count to get rid of the fear. Count... Ten, eleven, twelve, thirteen, fourteen... Breathing heavily. A hand touched his arm. Mostyn behind him.

'Feeling queasy, old Boysie boy?'

'Get knotted.'

'Oh, Boysie.' Cooing. 'Mustn't lose our sense of proportion. She frightened it away. Miss Muffet frightened the spider away with all that screaming.'

'What a sense of proportion? It's fun for you, isn't it? A good story to tell the chaps. You sadistic bastard.'

'Watch it, Boysie.'

'A bloody good yarn. Watching a girl getting her arse beaten to shreds then pegged down naked while a blasted great spider crawls all over her.'

'It's war, Boysie. That's our kind of show business.'

'War?'

'Never been colder, sport.'

'You talk about the red menace, the yellow peril, the sky-bloody-blue-pink terror; the big ogre knocking on the gates of freedom. Well, what the hell d'you think this is, you sordid old creeper? The little nightmare going on in there? Democracy? Christ you'd be the first to howl wouldn't you? First in the queue to moan about brutal atrocities? Come to think of it you did didn't you? You gave flaming evidence.' He remembered a conversation, only a few weeks ago. Mostyn talking with compassion about Belsen and Buchenwald.

'At Nuremburg. Yes.'

'Against *her* daddy's mates. And you allow her to carry on like that. What are you? A psychiatrist or something? Giving her psychotherapy? The woman's a ... a...'

'Sado-masochist?'

'Sado-whatever you say. Well that's it. I've finished. Bloody done. You. The Department. The whole bleeding issue. You can take it and stuff it up your union jacksies.' Terminus. Boysie had been boiling up for this all through the long winter. But Mostyn was experienced in dealing with his protégé's paddies.

'Don't get sentimental with me, Oakes.' Loud. Poisonous. Uncompromising.

Boysie's rage, hatred of the whole security system, his job, his gullibility, his private terror, had all blown out, leaving him a panting rag against the wall bars of the gymnasium. Mostyn was opening his mouth for another spate. Boysie had the foolish premonition that Mostyn was going to turn into a PTI shouting, 'Top of the wall bars– Go! Back again not quick enough.'

Mostyn's hesitation was only momentary. The voice sliced, cut and hacked into Boysie. 'Be your age, lad. There's no such thing as a goodie or a baddie any more. Haven't you learned that yet? Just people. Only people. People in opposition to one another. And very soon it'll only be survivors.' A pause. Snap of the fingers, the rat-eyes never leaving Boysie's face. Mostyno the Great Hypnotist. 'It's big, Boysie. So bloody big that most of the world doesn't realise what's happening. So complicated that you can't tell the difference between good or bad. Not any more – it simply depends on which side of the camera you happen to be standing at a given moment. And when Man's at stake what the hell does it matter if a girl's bottom get sore. Or if any itsy-bitsy spider climbs up her spout? So don't get sentimental with me, matey. The dusk of history, Boysie, that's where we're standing, in the dusk of history, and it's no place for consciences.'

Klara was coming through the doors, Angela and Martin trailing behind her like a couple of gun dogs. She began to speak as they crossed the gymnasium, half-way to Mostyn and Boysie.

'Tonight.' Surprisingly there was no sense of urgency. 'Tonight they're coming in. To coincide with the firework display.'

'Fireworks?' queried Mostyn.

'Yes, sir.' Martin playing teacher's pet. 'To launch the season. They do it every year, now and in August. Big firework display on the lake in front of Locarno.'

Klara was still talking. 'About quarter to midnight. The plan is to make a landing on the large island, through the island villa, force everyone out of the tunnels back into *Il Portone* and blow the underground complex – maybe put time-fused firebombs in *Portone* itself. I think she's telling the truth. She was to guide them in.'

'What you suspected.' Boysie to Mostyn. 'Irreparable damage. Complete disruption of training.'

Mostyn took no notice of the obvious comment. 'How many of them?'

'She's not sure. About twenty she thinks. But I'm not particularly worried, Colonel.' Klara looked smug. 'When they constructed the finer points of this place they built-in certain protective devices. They've been kept in working order, and even the talented Ingrid could know nothing about them. If Assault One attack from the lake they will regret it.'

'May have changed their minds, of course.' Mostyn turning into an astute tactician. 'Boysie's pinched their hovercraft for a start. They must know we're alerted. On the other hand they don't necessarily know we've got Ingrid.' He sucked his teeth noisily. 'Trouble is it couldn't have come at a worse time. Just before midnight.'

'Amber Nine?' Klara's eyebrows arched upwards.

'Scheduled for midnight isn't it?'

Klara nodded. 'It's a nasty coincidence. We must be thankful that Ingrid wasn't in on that. At least Assault One's action is independent of Amber Nine.'

The cry game from somewhere at the back of Angela's throat. It had the effect of a Gorgon's look – a rigid tension as Klara and the three men turned towards her. She had one hand to her mouth, incisors clamping down on the fleshy base of her thumb. The tweeny who had just shattered madam's treasured Spode.

'I told her, I didn't realise. She knew what it was...'

Instant spring from Klara, a hand clawing up, twisting the blonde hair and dragging the head back. 'Fool. What...?'

'I didn't know. She was my friend. She was so interested, and after Professor Skidmore explained...'

The deep freeze from Mostyn. 'Is she trying to say that Ingrid knew the extent of Amber Nine?'

'She is my head girl. I have reason to trust her.' Klara on the borderline of defending the tall girl. 'I thought it would be good experience. She was due to come to you, Special Security, next month. Skidmore gave permission for her to see the apparatus, there was even talk of her assisting with the recovery.' She heaved painfully on the hair. 'What did you tell Ingrid?'

'What Professor Skidmore said. What he told me. About the *Chronic Illness*. How they were going to get it down.'

Klara made a disgusted noise and twisted her hand, in a short arc, and with some force. The girl fell sideways, bumping heavily on the floor, sliding a foot or so.

'Get down to your quarters. Speak to no one. Wait for me there. You're an imbecile.

Finished.' She stepped out towards the door.

Mostyn beckoned Boysie and Martin with a sharp, annoyed, flap of the hand. 'How much did she know?'

'Enough. The essential details.' Klara over her shoulder, breaking through the doors like a gunfighter bursting into the Golden Nugget Saloon.

The three Seniors had just finished dressing Ingrid, propping her against the horse like a shop window dummy. Klara's voice all fury and viciousness.

'Down with her again. Get the grasshoppers. My whip – the bull-whip. She hasn't told us everything. There's more to come, Little Miss Muffet, isn't there?'

Ingrid was past caring. 'What? What is it? Anything. I'll tell you anything, just leave me alone.'

Klara was close to her, hands around her wrists, twisting so that they shook. Twisting like a school bully. 'This morning Angela gave you some information. She gave you details about Amber Nine.'

'Yes. Yes, she did. You didn't ask me before. Let go. Please.'

It was playground stuff.

'Have you transmitted any of that information?'

'I passed it on. Yes.' Ingrid panting, shivering.

'To whom.' Mostyn close to her now. Boysie felt definitely underprivileged. He still had no inkling of Amber Nine's scope.

'They gave me a telephone number to ring in case of emergencies.'

'Across the lake. The group headquarters?'

'No. Locarno.'

'Come on then. The number.'

'Locarno – that's code 093 – 093 24.46.70.'

'Damn.' Mostyn fumbling for the right decision. 'Can't use the police. Martin?'

'Sir?' Very military, pushing forward behind Boysie.

'How's your Italian?'

'Parla Inglese? I'm afraid.'

'Oh my god. From the whole Department I have to get lumbered with you and Boysie. Do your best. Get into Locarno and check that number. Try to eliminate the contact. Any trouble beat it – first train to Zürich and England. Right?'

'Do what I can, sir.'

'You armed?'

Martin patted his jacket affirmatively.

'One of the girls had better go with him,

Colonel.' Klara anxious to redress the harm done by Angela. 'Heather is fully trained. Heather?'

'Yes, Principal.'

Heather was jet-haired, with revitalised statistics.

'Better put some clothes on, hadn't she?' Mostyn eyeing the leather short-shorts.

'I don't really mind the informality,' said Martin cheerfully.

'All right,' Mostyn capitulated. 'Now for Professor Skidmore.'

Hector was scratching away in his nest. The noise made Boysie double uneasy. If it had not been for Hector he would have felt reasonably at peace with the world in Klara's study. The velvet drapes gave the impression of curtained windows, and the room now assumed an atmosphere of safety. What was more, Boysie enjoyed watching Klara and Mostyn beat their breasts. Klara made a short telephone call the moment the door was closed. ('Professor Skidmore? I'm sorry to bother you but I have two gentlemen here from Special Security. I think you'd better see them. Shall we come up, or will you come down to my study? You will. Good.') Sitting at her desk, Klara fell to cursing her own incompetence – for having appointed a head girl like Angela, whose notion of Security seemed only to mean 'a safe income and strong elastic': and for letting Ingrid wriggle through her net of security.

Mostyn also looked worried – slumped in thought, in the chair to which Boysie had been strapped during his last dramatic visit to the study. Mostyn seemed to be ticking off imaginary lists on his fingers. Finally:

'Let's go over what we've got already. Assault One are mounting a destructive operation against the school. Around midnight as far as we know. You say you can handle this?'

'Easily.'

'How much help?'

'Very little. Perhaps Cyril and Frederick – they're not one hundred per cent fit, thanks to Boysie, but we'll manage. Maybe a few of the girls down near the water. There are various mechanical controls on the top floor of the island villa. The whole place, you probably know, was designed as a bolthole. First for the man I called Uncle Benno, then for the pair of them – Uncle Benno and my beloved father. The builders did a good protection job. They were inclined to be nervous about their safety.'

'The hovercraft?'

'Frederick's moved it to the shore side of the island. I thought Professor Skidmore would want to use it for the recovery. We did have a speedboat.' She looked accusingly at Boysie who was still feeling very much out of the conversation.

'All right,' said Mostyn. 'I'll leave the defence to you. Now what about Amber Nine?'

'What *about* Amber Nine?' Boysie thought it was time to squawk. 'Look I'm implicated. Will somebody tell me? What is flipping Nine?'

Both Mostyn and Klara turned frozen faces towards him. Essence of wither. When Mostyn spoke, his voice was saturated with exaggerated weariness, a trick that infuriated Boysie. 'Do I have to?' He fingered his tie. A sigh. 'I suppose so. Are you sitting comfortably? Then I'll begin.'

'If you're going to take that attitude...'

'In our organisation there is a small, but apparently deadly department called Strategic Intelligence. They've been left pretty much to themselves, but – according to our Chief, whose judgment I trust – they've acquitted themselves with distinction.' This was the old pompous Mostyn, stopping to squint down the elegant crease in his trouser leg. Talking slowly, explaining to a small child. 'Strategic Intelligence has, as its nucleus, a team of scientists. Their Chief is Professor Skidmore. Well, Boysie, you know scientists. No head for routine. Within his cranium old Skidmore probably holds more secrets than any one man in Security. But he's inclined to be a bit hazy about procedure. Anyway, that's another part of the tale. Old Uncle Skidmore has come across some basic development in cold war ploys and...'

The knock at the door was heavy and demanding.

'I think it will be better for the Professor to explain things himself,' said Klara, adding a loud 'Come in.'

He was an elderly colossus. A six-footer who, at nearly seventy, had only the mildest hint of a stoop. His hair, once fire-red, now splashed with grey, gave the appearance of being badly dyed and left to grow back into its natural state. The gingery hopsack suit looked as though it had been put together by a couple of lads trained in the mailbag room at the Scrubs. The hands were large, clumsy and red like some old washerwoman's. He wore thick heavy-lensed glasses with tortoise-shell frames, clamped on to a beakish nose which made him look as though he was wearing some joke disguise for a child's Christmas stocking.

'Good afternoon, Doctor. These the gentlemen?' A voice rich, and savouring of a port laid down well in a good year. For all his clownish appearance the man commanded immediate respect – a natural leader, decisive, and with obvious intellect. Boysie and Mostyn were both on their feet.

'Professor Skidmore.' Klara, deferential. 'May I introduce Colonel Mostyn and Mr Oakes.'

The old chap nodded affably.

'We're from Special Security,' said Mostyn in his no-beating-about-the-bush voice.

'I see. May I have your credentials?'

Mostyn brought out his passport. Boysie remembered his was still back at the hotel and made noises at Mostyn meant to communicate that fact.

'I'll vouch for Oakes,' said Mostyn, back to the weary note and slipping a wait-till-I-get-you-alone look at his underling.

'I'm a scientist by trade.' The professor briskly took the passport and opened it. 'But I'm getting used to your cloak and dagger ways. Let me see. Page four. *Valid for all parts of the Commonwealth and for all Foreign Countries.* Special Security you say? The s in Countries should be out of alignment – which it is. Thank you Colonel.'

The passport was returned.

'I'm afraid I've got some rather serious news.' Mostyn doing his best to be politic.

'It's a rather serious world. Shoot.' Skidmore was surprisingly hip.

'First of all, sir, I'd better tell you that the Director of Supreme Control's not too happy about Amber Nine.'

'He will be when he gets my report.'

Boysie considered how small Mostyn looked next to the giant superbrain.

'Maybe, sir. But you didn't mount the operation through the normal channels, did you?'

That's a laugh, thought Boysie. A remark like that coming from Mostyn – biggest red-tape trimmer in the business.

'Oh dear have I slipped up somewhere?' Skidmore's wide-eyed innocence was blatantly fake. 'NATO people seemed happy enough.'

Boysie was mentally cheering the Prof. He's sending him up, he thought, sending Mostyn up rotten.

'Yes, but you didn't get clearance through anyone else did you.' It was impossible for Mostyn to keep that edge of menace out of his voice.

'No, I suppose not.' The old boy chuckled to himself.

'It is usual to go through Supreme Control. All Departments should be advised of a major operation like this.'

Mostyn would do himself an injury if he went on like that.

'Why?'

'People ought to be put in the picture.'

'Absolute bloody nonsense. More people who know about it less chance there is of pulling it off.' It must have been galling to Mostyn. Skidmore was purposely playing the stiff-necked genius steamrolling authority with homespun logic.

'Anyway,' he continued, 'Old Fluffy Greenhaugh knew about it.'

'Chief of Training Command? Yes, of course he knew.'

'I was in a fix. Wanted a place in the right geographical location. Mentioned it to Fluffy – at school with my brother you know. Said he'd just the spot. Here. Ideal. Couldn't be better.'

'Yes, I gather that, sir. But, actually,

Training Command have been in error as well. This school operates on neutral territory. You're about to pull a stunt – a rather large stunt – on neutral territory.'

'Point taken. Old Fluffy on the mat, eh?' He looked benignly round the room. 'Couldn't put it through normal channels anyway. Nobody would've allowed me to do it. Had to play it chilly.'

'Thought you should be warned anyway, sir.'

'Good of you. Good of you. You will be remembered.' The last sentence ambiguous.

'There is more, sir. Serious developments I'm afraid.'

'Go ahead.' Skidmore eased himself into a chair and took out a clean, polished briar which he filled and lit with considerable care. The man fascinated Boysie. It was as though some great nursery teddy bear, a symbol of normality, had entered the half-world of confused fantasy which, until now, had clouded the experiences of the past two days.

Mostyn was lucid. Sticking to essentials, he outlined the situation which had brewed since Boysie had lumbered on to the scene. There was a full minute's silence after he stopped speaking.

'It's a blow.' Skidmore puffed on his pipe – a bloom of smoke obscuring the relief-map face. 'Can't deny it's a blow.' He held the bowl of the briar in his right hand and tapped his teeth with the stem. Boysie could see, by the look on Mostyn's face, that the mannerism irritated the Second-in-Command. 'Two obvious courses of action. The group – what d'ye call 'em? Assault One? They won't be so bothered about this.' He swung his hand in a semi-circle indicating the whole underlake complex. 'They're more likely to make for us – in the island villa. Knock out our control.'

'You needn't worry about that.' Klara from the desk. 'I've told the Colonel and Mr Oakes, if they come from the lake they won't get very far.'

'Good. But if by any chance they've got the information back – I mean right back – there are many things that can go wrong. They can alter frequencies. Change the vehicle. All our stuff will be useless.' He smacked his knee with the flat of his hand. 'Eight million quid's worth of electronics up there in the island villa, and if they simply alter the frequency it'll be about as much use as a transistor radio. Pchaach!' A sort of spitting noise. '*Less* use than a transistor, at least you'd be able to get the top ten on that.' He sat in silence for another minute 'Press on regardless. That's all we can do. Fireworks. Dramatic assaults. Commando raids. Guts ache. I just have to press on. Fingers crossed.'

'And prayer wheels at the steady turn.' Mostyn jaded.

'I wish somebody...' Started Boysie.

'Shut up,' muttered Mostyn.

'Tush now.' The big man like a scolding nanny. 'What is it, lad?' Playing the kindly uncle.

'Well,' said Boysie, almost belligerently. 'I just wish someone would put us entirely in the picture. Amber Nine I mean.'

'Ah.' Skidmore beamed. It was like asking an egotistical gardener to talk about his chrysanths. Amber Nine was built into the man's cardiac system. He shifted to a more comfortable position in the chair. The whisper of a sigh from Mostyn, then Skidmore was off.

'It begins,' he said, as comfortable as a children's storyteller. 'It begins with a question of tactics. We all know the tactical situation in Europe – developed into nothing more'n a brainy game. I know it. You know it. This fellow at the Hudson Institute

– where they waste their time thinking about instant disaster. Kahn. Herman Kahn. Nuclear strategist. Invented escalation and plays war games with the top brass. Games. He's got sense that chap. Reduced the whole damn thing to a game of chess. And that's all it amounts to. A bloody great game of nuclear chess. H-bombs. Missiles. Weapons. They're no more than a threat than my arse – if you'll pardon the expression, ma'am.' A gracious look towards Klara who giggled. 'They may terrorise the man in the street – almost certainly do, judging by their faces when the Press yells crisis. But, in my opinion, the true value of nuclear weapons is negative and as outdated as the battering ram. It's checkmate. They all know it. Lyndon Johnson knows it. That fellow what's his name? Fellow in Downing street.'

Mostyn mentioned the name of the Prime Minister.

'That's the chap. He knows it.' Skidmore lifted himself out of the chair and took the centre of the floor. 'Point about nuclear weapons – the nuclear arms race – is that it has balanced power too finely. And in order to live within that balance we exist in a continual state bordering on Condition

Blue. You've heard of Condition Blue?'

'Lowest state of readiness.' Boysie had read *Fail Safe,* and seen the movie.

'Lowest state. It means the missile bases are on a twenty-four hour alert, that the NATO V-Force can get into the air in a matter of minutes; and it means that prescribed areas are patrolled by Strategic Air Command – little men in big aeroplanes carrying the real thing. The Bomb.' He made a gesture with his hands.

Miming the Bomb, thought Boysie, was very close to miming the contours of a beautiful woman. Skidmore was speaking again.

'And, of course, the same applies to the opposition. The DA – Dalnaya Aviatsiya their equivalent of SAC – patrols strictly delineated air corridors. Carrying the Weapon as well.' He allowed the point to sink home before coming to his big punch. 'Only, in the last year there has been a subtle swing in the balance of power. Every hour of every day the DA has exactly sixty aircraft, airborne and on patrol. Twenty of those aeroplanes do *not* carry the Bomb. Their load is something quite different. Something our research teams have been working at since Hiroshima. Something which so swings the balance of power that the Herman Kahns of this world haven't yet taken it into account.'

Though Klara and Mostyn already knew what was coming, Skidmore's total involvement, his command and manner, held them in complete concentration. The Professor rummaged in the vast pockets of his baggy hopsack and unearthed a silver ballpoint, holding it in front of him delicately in his vast paws, the pipe stem between his teeth making little noticeable difference to his speech.

'Physically, it's like a large version of the old Nazi V1– the Doodle-bug. The Flying Bomb. A pilotless aircraft. Delivery vehicle. Rocket power in the tail, stubby delta wings, long bullet-shaped body.' The pen was a stand-in for the weapon. He walked over to Klara's desk – shifting a piece of paper: a white oblong centred on the polished surface. 'Target.' With a nod towards the paper. His eyes skimmed the desk again and he pounced on a paper clip.

'The thing,' he waggled the pen, 'just fits nicely underneath their Tupolev TU-20. The Mark B – the one we code Bear-B. Carries it where they normally sling the Kangaroo stand-off missile. With their usual flair for dark humour they call this one *ostraye zabalevaheeye* – roughly translated means *Chronic illness*. We know they have at least forty such weapons. Twenty of them always in the air.'

'*Chronic illness...*' Boysie was on the edge of his chair.

'Nose-cone holds computer and electronic brain. Fuel in the rear – dramatic system that gives it a range of over 1,500 miles. Five times as great as the *Kangaroo*. Small centre section is the guts. Whole thing's an absolute triumph. When they release it, the vehicle soars straight up to around 60,000 feet – normal operational height till it approaches the target.' He held the pipe and pen close together, moving them along – the aircraft in flight. One hand dropped away with the pen then moved upwards, the hand with the pipe continuing in simulated level flight. 'Aircraft keeps on course for ten minutes, then turns away. Come to the reason for that later.' His eyes rested on the pen, held high in his right fist, the thumb and forefinger lightly clamping the paper clip.

'It's going at a speed of around 6,000 mph, reducing slightly as it vectors on to the target, drops and passes over at about 20,000 feet.' He brought the pen down over

306

the desk.

'Immediately over the target it drops its own weapon.' The pipe was back in his mouth, left hand coming up to grab the paper clip which he pulled away, slowly bringing it down over the piece of paper.

'Delivery vehicle lifts its nose and goes straight up at speed and finally disintegrates. Tiny pieces. Phhuff.' The pen raised in the right hand and then disposed to a pocket. Attention now on the paper clip. 'It has dropped a canister about the size of an oil drum which bursts open at around three to four thousand feet. Inside there are three smaller canisters. The contents of these canisters amalgamate just before the explosion, under pressure, and the resultant particles are shot away – in all directions – at an extraordinary velocity. Billions, trillions, quadrillions of them. A cloud finer than dust. Undetectable to the human eye.' He dropped the paper clip into the middle of the paper, puffed on his pipe and blew a mouthful of smoke down on to the desk. 'Depending on weather conditions and height of release, the particles can spread over a radius of two hundred miles.' The big hand inscribed a circle round the desk. 'Two hundred, and that's an optimistic figure. In our favour.'

'What do they do for crying out loud?' From Boysie.

'That's exactly what we want to find out.' Skidmore was back in his chair. His manner changed to that of a scholarly lecturer. 'Strange, the other day I came across a passage written by Thomas Willis – seventeenth-century surgeon. Actually writing about 'flu in 1659. What he said was: *Suddenly a Distemper arose, as if sent by some blast of the stars, which laid hold on very many together: that in some towns, in the space of a week, about a thousand people fell together.* The *Chronic Illness* is a bit like that but more so. We know it'll cause a tremendously virile fever. We know it attacks at great speed – matter of ten or twenty minutes after contact. We know it is both highly infectious and contagious. The Asian 'Flu epidemic of 1957 was probably a very mild try out of a similar, though less violent, virus which got a little out of hand. We know they've perfected protection against it – a vaccine. And we know, positively, that it will spread like the proverbial forest fire. For instance, one exploded over Birmingham would cripple the whole of the Midlands in a matter of hours; the whole of Britain in a day. Just imagine a country where ninety-nine out of every hundred people were sweating, with temperatures around the 104 mark, and blinding headaches. Total paralysis. Transport, industry, government, defence, everything.'

'Wouldn't it have been easier to go for the jack-pot?' Mostyn a shade too suave. 'Get the vaccine?'

'You think we haven't tried?' Dismissive.

'It seems strange that you've been able to get hold of so much information on the weapon and yet not latch on to the really important thing.'

'You *are* a professional security man?' asked Skidmore patiently.

Mostyn managed to keep back his anger. 'Since the beginning of World War II.'

'Then you know about strategic leaks – information let out deliberately?'

Mostyn took a deep, rage-impregnated breath.

'Ninety per cent of the stuff we've already got has been handed to us on a plate.' Skidmore making the words into short jabs at Mostyn's stomach. 'We know practically everything there is to know about this damn thing, except the ingredients – the contents of those three canisters, and how they fuse together, and what they make when mixed. There've been one or two inspired guesses, but they've turned out to be bloody nonsense.' He leaned forward, emphasising his point by shaking the top half of his body in a low jerky rhythm. 'Mind you we are not completely *au fait* with all the technicalities – fuel system's a bloody miracle to begin with. But it's in their favour that we should know. And of course they don't want us to know the structure of the canisters – the virus, bacteria, or whatever is formed. But now...' He rubbed his hands smartly together with a sizzling sound. 'But now we have 'em by the hip.'

'The hip.' Repeated Boysie, hypnotised by the scientist's easy manner of one-up-Mostynmanship.

'The opposition also has their form of fail safe,' continued Skidmore, his face beaming with intrigue – a small boy counting a secret hoard of goodies. 'Particularly with this weapon. For instance, the disintegrating device is built into the metal. It goes off at a certain height to destroy after the main canister has been dropped. It also destroys – with the canister – if approached by a missile. What's more important, it's computer-controlled – from the ground. They won't even allow their pilots the responsibility of launching.'

'All done by tape,' murmured Mostyn.

'As you say. Each weapon has its own frequency and reacts to taped bleeps fed onto its electronic system from a VHF transmitter. The pilot only knows he's carried out a mission when the aircraft suddenly gets lighter and a bulb flashes on his instrument panel. Not going into all the technical difficulties – much too complicated – but what happens is that the bleeped orders are transmitted from their ground control, through electronic equipment to the aircraft, to the weapon's brain. The pilot holds his course, at a set speed, for ten minutes after launching in case of emergency changes. And I can tell you they've got all emergencies taped – literally. If there's an accidental launching, ground control switches to another tape and either sends the thing up to disintegration height, or re-routes it out to sea. It's happened as well. Six months ago some fellow threw the wrong switch in their ground control and the *Chronic Illness* was heading for Rome. My God. Virus in the Vatican. They'd have screamed for the Pill.' Skidmore stopped, took out his matches, slowly relit his pipe, looked at the burning match for a moment then extinguished the flame by throwing it over his shoulder, immediately stuffing his fingers into his ears and grimacing, like one expecting a bomb-blast. Boysie hooted and the Professor joined in – Friar Tuck, Father Christmas and the Jolly Miller all rolled into one. Mostyn forced a smile. Klara looked amazed.

'Didn't reach Rome, of course. They ran the emergency tape, locks went on – they have safety-locks for the main canister – and the *Chronic Illness* ended up slap bang in the middle of the Adriatic.'

'And…?' asked Boysie.

'And what?'

'And how have we got them by the hip?'

'Oh that. We've picked up a bunch of control tapes.' Skidmore chuckling. 'One of our more enterprising operatives – chap called Phentos – took a risk which paid off. Three months ago we got the control tapes for *Chronic Illness UR/39*. Deciphered them. Made our own control tapes for *UR/39* and put eight million nickers' worth of bloody complicated equipment into Doctor Thirel's attic. Tonight *UR/39* will be on patrol along the Yugoslavian corridor between Dubrovnik and Split. We transmit the release signal

312

and target instructions. Target Five: Genoa – just as though the weapon was being unleashed by their control. Within two seconds of release we send a second series of signals, changing the operating frequency – putting their ground control right out of the picture. For a minute or so, *Chronic Illness UR/39* will be all set to worry Genoa's Medical Officer of Health. Then our final series of signals puts the locks on and redirects the vehicle for a splash-down here. On Maggiore.' He beamed at Boysie. A child who knows it has said something cute. 'If our tapes are accurate, it should end up around six hundred yards from the Isole di Brissago.'

As a technocrat Boysie Oakes was no great shakes. He could mend a fuse, but would be unable to tell you what part the fuse played in the system of things. Innocently he accepted the march of scientific progress as magic. If they told him a missile could be activated from a control two, three, four, five thousand miles away, and brought down on a pin point he would believe them – and remain unhappy. Boysie lived mainly on a physical plain, and Skidmore had so fascinated his jumbled mind that it now held a series of highly coloured, vivid pictures. Trains standing in lonely stations with passengers lolling out of the windows; deserted highways; silent cities, a door banging in the wind with nobody to close it; milk turning sour on the cat's saucer; whole countries lying on the rack of suffering; a plague leaping from the stars, riding an invisible beam, straddled on the back of a long black craft. In these terms, Boysie could see the dangers. He could even smell the scent of destruction. He knew why Skidmore cut corners and how important it was to get the canisters. Now he could see *Chronic Illness UR/39* in slow motion against dark mountains, swooping like a diseased black swan on to the lake.

'And once it's in the water.' Aloud, pleased he had at least followed the gist of Skidmore's explanation. 'All you have to do is nip out and get the canisters.'

'Well, I don't.' Skidmore rumbled a belly laugh. 'Getting too old and fat for that. Me senior assistant, Fortescue, is too old and thin. But I've got a first rate junior – Russell Palfreyman. Dab hand with the old frogman suit. He'll go out in a boat. We've got a mock-up of a *Chronic Illness* in the island villa. Russell can remove the whole trinity of canisters in a matter of ten minutes. Should

give him ample time. We've got thirty minutes after the vehicle hits the water before it
blows.'

Boysie quickly went over the whole
operation in his mind. Something puzzled
him. It had nothing to do with electronics,
beams, computers, radar, or germ warfare.

'Could you explain one thing, Professor?'

'Certainly, my boy.' Cheerful Uncle
Skidmore.

'What the devil's Amber Nine got to do
with it?'

'Didn't I tell you? We've called the
operation Amber Nine because· we're re-
routing *UR/39* along the first leg of the
commercial air lane known as A90 – Amber
Nine. Runs from Genoa across the Voghera
beacon to the Monte Ceneri beacon here,
then on through Zürich, Stuttgart...' He was
cut short by the telephone coming to life on
Klara's desk. She answered it, covered the
mouthpiece and looked at Skidmore.

'You're wanted in the Control Room,
Professor, they say it's urgent.'

'Oh?' Grumpy. 'Do they now? We'd best
all go. You can have a look at my toys.' This
last to Boysie.

Mostyn and Klara led the way. Boysie
tagging behind with Skidmore. As they

turned into the main passage the Professor took Boysie's arm and spoke in a low voice.

'That chap – what's his name? Other security fellow? Frostin? What?'

'Mostyn. Colonel Mostyn,' corrected Boysie.

'Bit dim isn't he? Strange sort of chap.'

Boysie jumped at the opportunity. 'He's getting on a bit, sir. Seen a lot of action. Mustn't be too hard on him.'

'Funny chap. Very strange chap indeed.'

Kadjawaji liked *grappa* – that pernicious liquor which is virtually the dregs and residue from the distillation of brandy. To Kadjawaji, *grappa* was a delicacy normally difficult to obtain. Here he could drink his fill. Carefully he poured the colourless fluid from his liqueur glass into a *demi tasse* of thick coffee. A minute finger and thumb closed round the cup's handle. A sip. A pleased expression. The two men and the girl, watching from the other side of the room, all felt a flicker of irritation. They did not particularly care for Kadjawaji, but they were professionals doing a job. Kadjawaji came with the job. They wished, however, that he would stop dramatising – playing the mastermind. They knew his reputation but –

if this morning's panic was anything to go by – the dwarf was deteriorating.

A second sip. Another smile. Then the piping voice. A violin badly tuned. 'I require the whole group – all members of Assault One – up here at three o'clock. There are to be some slight modifications to our landing procedure.'

One of the men moved as if to leave.

'I've not yet finished.' A big deal screech. Then, more controlled, 'The local operative from Locarno – the one who's been acting as our radio link. The one we have not yet been allowed to meet. He's received instructions. He will be coming with us tonight. Details later.'

Another sip of coffee, and the tiny man slid from his chair – an agile monkey, or some terribly deformed child.

'You may go.' Arrogant.

Sullenly the three group members left the room. Kadjawaji opened the windows and stumped out on to the terrace which formed the top of the boathouse. He stood for five minutes, his eyes straining across the lake in the direction of the Isole di Brissago.

Across the Continent, Major Tusykov looked out of the crew-room window. It was always a bleak time of day – just before they began the long patrol. The hours of concentration. Out on the apron the ground staff were making final adjustments to 05 – his TU-20. NATO had code-named the TU-20, *Bear*. A good name for this monster – unique in its field, the only turbo-jet strategic bomber combining aircrews and a swept-wing design. In fact, the only turbo-jet strategic bomber in service with any air arm.

Tusykov was more than usually nervous today. The Commandant had given strict instructions that they were to remain in the crew-room until summoned to the aircraft by telephone. Usually they wandered out among the ground staff. It eased the tension. Major Tusykov recalled that the tension had never seemed so bad when they were carrying the *Kangaroo* missile. It was since their role had altered he had sensed a change in himself and the others. Perhaps it was because they never felt completely in control when patrolling with the *Chronic Illness*. There were half-a-dozen technicians from the laboratories working on the weapon now, scurrying in and out underneath the aircraft. They too had been edgy – especially since the incident last year when

UR/25 went shooting off towards Rome.

Tusykov shrugged and looked away from the aircraft, over the field to the small dot of concrete that was the control bunker. Inside they would now be tracking 04 which carried *UR/29*. That was Illovych. Good pilot. He would be making his final turn before the long retracing return. Inside the bunker they would also be preparing the tapes for the weapon firmly clamped to the belly of Tusykov's *Bear. UR/39.*

A mile or so on past the control bunker Tusykov could see the tips of the rocket testing gantries. Funny how the wind moaned through the great metal skeletons. It was a sound which persisted in this place. A moan like the cries from a large number of sick people.

Klara led them straight up the main passage, past the intersection – which branched off to Seniors' quarters on one side, and cells on the other – to the large steel vault door which brought the central underground corridor to a dead end. Earlier Boysie had not been close enough, to the door to make any thorough examination. Now he saw it lay flush with the wall – no sign of any hinges, handles or bolts. Just a flat shining slab of steel with a tiny perforated circle, the size of a penny, in the centre.

'Let me,' said the Professor, arms doing the crawl to get past Klara and Mostyn. 'Always liked working this thing.' He stood close to the door, lips near the perforated circle.

'Five, four, two, eight. A stroke CX. Open says me.' The door slid upward revealing a lift cage.

'Don't really need the "open says me",' grinned Skidmore to Boysie. 'Me own bit of nonsense. You get it? Open says me. Open sesame. Alladin.' Guffaw.

'Very comical, Professor. Popeye does it as well.' Mostyn without feeling. Skidmore looked at Boysie and mouthed a silent, 'Strange bloke.'

The lift took them up into the island villa – out on to a staircase landing: empty, bare walls, creaking floorboards, a silt of dust. Boysie had the impression of vast ante-rooms, chambers, alcoves, halls and long passages, a rustle of the eighteenth century; far below, over the banisters, a tiled floor. Cobwebs. It was a ridiculous place for an operation as totally contemporary as this,

'Only way into our humble little dwelling,'

said Skidmore indicating the lift. 'Doors and windows all sealed off with steel shutters.'

'They would have to scale the walls – some of the upper windows are accessible They could get in by climbing the walls.' Klara, pausing by a door.

They went through into a big, square, high room – literally filled with a radar scanner, its massive metal bowl looking ludicrously out of place.

'They don't seem this large sitting on the edge of an airfield do they?' Mostyn was leaning back, impressed for a change.

'Works on a lift. Straight through the roof. Had to get the floor and walls reinforced,' explained the Professor. 'Once it's up and turning we're in business. Only shove it up at night – like the conservatives, eh? Might frighten the locals to see a damn great thing like that whizzing round on top of the house.'

There was room to walk round the scanner to the next door, which opened before they reached it. A shrunken weed of a man came out. A dehydrated human being. A body of bone and loose skin terminating in a sharp, wrinkled face with whispy white hair.

'Oh, Professor. I'm so glad you've returned

sir. So glad. This is more unfortunate. Most. I warned him. Be careful, Russell, I said...'

Skidmore raised one hand. The thin whinny of chatter stopped as though someone had sliced through the aged one's vocal chords.

'This is Fortescue. Been with me almost since I graduated. Me regular old scrotum – the wrinkled retainer, what?'

Boysie and Mostyn thought Fortescue was going to have a funny turn. He seemed to fold in two and then spring sharply back again, rocking on his heels. A strained cackle emitted from between the almost non-existent lips.

'Always cheers him up that one. Now, my old. What's to do,' said Skidmore.

'Ye'd better come in, Professor. See what you can do. Really I tried to stop him. These young men. These foolish young men. Mods and Rockers. Mods and Rockers...' Fortescue was toddling back from whence he had come, the little head shaking violently.

'I wonder,' said Mostyn, to no one in particular, 'how Strategic Intelligence managed to get him on their strength?'

The movement which Skidmore performed was as near as he could ever come to doing a *fouetté*. No trace of humour across the lumpy features as he faced Mostyn. 'Fortescue,' he said, like doom's crack, 'is my most valuable man. What he knows about radio, electronics, radar and the like would – if printed in very small type – fill enough books to stock the entire shelf space of the British Museum Library. Yes, and the Brooklyn Public Library as well.' He took two paces through the door and turned again with an after-thought. 'You could possibly include the Folger Library in Washington. He's a brilliant old man. I'd be grateful if you would remember that and kindly keep your comments to yourself.'

This, thought Boysie, is what it will be like if they drop the Bomb. He followed Mostyn through the door. The Second-in-Command's shoulders were set as though in concrete.

No trace of the dusty past remained in the room. The inevitable strip-lights replaced windows. Shining hygienic walls and a floor covered with some dust-proof plastic material. Along one wall a work bench sagged with tools and an untidy collection of electronic accoutrements. The wall facing them was almost completely covered by an opaque screen, like some mammoth television – switched off at the moment, dull grey. Below it, more apparatus – steel-enclosed and, to Boysie, a meaningless battery of complexities. In the centre of the room stood a large computer consol. On either side, a pair of upright radar indicator screens and their controls. On the floor, in front of the computer, a young man lay in a position of extreme pain. His body squeezed into a dry-type diving suit, twisted at an unnatural angle. The face, sporting a slightly Semetic aspect, had turned to that shade of parchment green which denotes considerable physical agony.

'Russell, my dear boy. What have you done?' Skidmore kneeling beside the luckless Russell Palfreyman, his junior assistant.

'My leg,' said Russell, teeth gritting. Klara moved in close, her hands feeling the bones through the rubber with undoubted medical efficiency.

'I warned him. He would go sky-larking in that suit. With the fins on. Hooligan. Mod. Rocker.' Fortescue hopping from one foot to another as though in urgent need of the nearest *Gents.*

'But how on earth?' Skidmore's great head rolling from side to side like an angry bull.

'Tripped over my flippin' flippers,' said

Russell. 'Just getting acclimatised and tripped over my flippers.'

'Skylarking. I warned you.' Fortescue going great guns.

'I'm afraid there is a fracture. Nasty. Compound by the feel.' Klara looked up, her hands still pressing on the damaged leg.

'Aaaargh,' said Russell loudly – *con vivo*.

'This complicates things. Russ was the boy retriever. Canister picker-upper I seem to recall.' Mostyn, pleased to the point of applause.

Boysie deduced that Mostyn was not altogether in tune with the work of Strategic Intelligence.

'Indeed,' said Skidmore, getting to his feet. 'We'll need someone else for the recovery. Someone to go out and get the canisters. Someone...'

'None of my girls are going.' Klara quickly squashing any half-formed ideas. 'After the business with Ingrid, and then Angela's abominable lack of Security, I couldn't be responsible. And neither Frederick nor Cyril are fit enough to handle anything like this.'

'We need,' said Skidmore slowly, 'somebody who is reasonably fit. A moderate swimmer – in case of accidents. One who is intelligent enough to be taught the routine within the next few hours.'

Boysie became aware that Professor Skidmore was looking straight at him. He glanced round in case someone stood behind him. Nobody did. Mostyn was looking at him – an unholy light in those piggy eyes. Now Fortescue and Klara.

'Good luck, mate,' groaned Russell.

'No.' Boysie backed towards the door. 'No. No. NO.'

CHAPTER TWELVE

AMBER NINE: LAKE MAGGIORE

'Frogman.' Boysie, tightly encased, like a *paupiette de veau*, in the black rubber diving suit, was boiling up to high sulking point.

'"Here's-a-pistol-for-the-Rat, here's-a-pistol-for-the-Mole, here's-a-pistol-for-the-Toad, here's-a-pistol-for-the-Badger."' Quoted Mostyn. 'Apt old Boysie. Type casting. Toad.' He looked across the room to where Skidmore sat in front of the consol. 'Badger. And Mole.' Indicating Fortescue, running around the equipment like a whirling dervish.

'And Rat,' said Boysie, right between Mostyn's eyes. 'Wind in the flaming Willows. I've been wearing this king-size contraceptive since four. One pee, and that took ten minutes.'

'We don't want you getting wet, old son. Stop feeling sorry for yourself, I've been working as well. We're both involved.'

Boysie admitted this was true. After the

injured Palfreyman had been removed – seven hours before – Mostyn revealed that he had once done a week's course on hovercraft. The rest followed as naturally as indigestion to a surfeit of boiled onions, Mostyn was taken off to the hovercraft, while Skidmore and Fortescue led Boysie into the basement. Some luxurious and over-flush previous owner had felt it necessary to provide the villa with an indoor swimming pool next to the wine cellar – a large pink and green monstrosity designed with all the flamboyant tastelessness of the *avant garde* 1930s. In the centre of the pool floated a full scale replica of the *Chronic Illness* missile – its long bullet body and tiny wings making it look suspiciously like a vehicle filched from a fairground Jet Plane ride. It took Boysie an hour to master the technique of lying across a stubby wing, hanging on with one hand and operating his screwdriver with the other – the water making the aluminium skin as negotiable as a greasy pole.

Then there was the long routine for the removal of the canisters – inspection plate (eight screws) off on either side, a similar plate on the drum inside the fuselage; uncoupling twelve terminals in strict rotation; unscrewing the canister nearest to him; then the forward canister; swim round to the other side; off with the two plates to get at the third canister. Practice. Practice. Boysie went through it again and again – Skidmore offering advice and Fortescue joining in with 'That's the way, Boysie. Practice makes perfect. Damn the Mods and Rockers. Unscrew. Unscrew...'

'Screw it,' shouted Boysie after the fifteenth rehearsal. But they went on.

Later, Mostyn came down looking pleased with himself, boasting that he could manage the hovercraft blindfold.

Together, they worked out a quick means of transporting the canisters from missile to hovercraft – with Mostyn passing down a short rope and sling. Through it all again – Skidmore at the stop watch and Mostyn simulating the pull up to the hovercraft's cockpit.

Mostyn disappeared, but Boysie went on. Screws. Screws. Terminals. Canisters. Swim. Screws. Canister. By nine o'clock he could do it in fifteen minutes.

'Call it twenty,' said Skidmore. 'It'll be more difficult getting the tins out while you're actually splashing around in the lake.'

'That only gives us ten minutes reserve for Chrissake.'

'Near thing. Going to be a near thing,' chattered ancient Fortescue.

At a final briefing it was decided that the hovercraft would be moored on the north side of the island – where Boysie, Petronella and stone-cold Lynne had stolen the speedboat. Boysie and Mostyn would stay in the computer room until there was no doubt *Chronic Illness UR/39* would make a successful splashdown. They would then go fast to the hovercraft and move out on to the lake – Skidmore giving them a fix and bearing by radio.

At nine thirty Boysie was allowed back into *Il Portone* to say goodbye to Petronella – now en route for London with Martin in attendance. Martin had returned to the school during the early evening, disenchanted, with news that he had located the Locarno telephone number in an empty flat in the Minuiso area. There was an automatic recording device on the phone, but the tape was new and unused. Ingrid's information on *Amber Nine* had definitely got to Locarno.

'See you in London, then,' said Boysie avoiding Petronella's eyes. They stood alone in the hall. Over her shoulder he could see Martin patiently pacing by the car in front of the house.

'If you'll give me your address and telephone number, Boysie.' Petronella put her hands on his shoulders. 'We've got that unfinished symphony to perform. Remember?'

They kissed. Friendly more than fierce – on account of the frogman suit. Petronella departed, sadly, but with full details of the flat off Chesham Place.

Food – Boysie picking at cold chicken and salad – in the deserted dining-room. The Virgins had all disappeared, and there was a definite sense of the decks being cleared. Mostyn joined him and, at ten thirty, Klara came up to take them back to the island villa. A Senior stood by the lift – leather shorts discarded for a black cat suit. She carried a Sten gun. Down the main underlake passage they passed three more Seniors – cat suited again, the leader with a Sten, the others belted with holsters holding unladylike 9 mm Super Stars. A far cry from the hockey and lax sticks of Roedean or Vassar. Once in the island villa Klara carted Mostyn away to see the defence preparations and the mechanical devices her

Uncle Benno had once built into the island.

Boysie was ordered to relax – in a small rest room (couch, chair, ashtray) leading off Skidmore's do-it-yourself Cape Kennedy Control Kit.

Since they had forced him into the rubber suit, Boysie's energy and concentration had been almost totally directed towards mastering the recovery routine. Now, alone on his back, trickling cigarette smoke up between his teeth, Boysie's mind was free to range over the forthcoming problems. Fear sharpened the imagination. Out of focus, the *Chronic Illness* missile bobbing on the lake expanded to the size of a ditched airliner, while the lake itself became a heavy Atlantic swell – a brewing storm with fifty-foot wave-troughs keeling the giant missile to and fro: Boysie like a fly trying to climb the wing.

Boysie took a deep breath. Just as quickly the picture righted itself. He could feel his hand on the screwdriver, steady, with the slight movement of the missile below. It was not a question of whether this whole business terrified him, or if it seemed ludicrous, impossible. Weapons like this existed. They were a threat to Boysie personally and to all the Boysies – male and female – who lived and breathed on this stinking planet. OK, his fear, spinelessness, lack of guts, was a personal matter. It was also the fear of millions – those terrified of losing the myth of democracy, and those frightened of the big bad giant democracy. He thought about this for a minute or so. Conclusions: to be afraid was not something of which he need be ashamed. It was true. But he did not help the drunken butterflies staggering through his gut, nor the thumping quake-beat of his heart. For the second time that day, Boysie yearned for comfort – physical if possible, sexual for preference. And, for the second time, the door opened on cue. He expected to see Petronella – broken free from Martin and returning to be at his side, to comfort his last moments. It was Angela.

'Coffee?' she said, putting the cup on the chair. Her eyes showed red rims under the careful make-up.

'Thanks. You all right?' Slow. Charming.

'Mm-hu.' Affirmative.

'Not going to be shot at dawn then?' Smooth man-of-the-world.

'No. I've been given another chance. Got to stay on for a year though.' Dismal.

'That's not so bad. Sit down for a minute.' Tongue hanging out.

'I don't think that would be very comfortable,' said Angela, backing towards the door, a flush breaking through the Rubinstein *French Beige*. 'Doctor Thirel's methods are old fashioned – and painful.'

Mostyn returned at eleven twenty.

'Right, old son. This is it.' Something of the execution chamber about the greeting. Boysie swung off the bed, zipped up the front of his jacket, buckled the straps of both sheath knife and tool kit around his thighs, and picked up the flippers – the inadvertent cause of his predicament.

'Radio link's good.' Mostyn sounded sweetly cheerful. 'Just checked it out. And wait until you see the tricks that Klara's got tucked away. Nasty minds, Uncle and Daddy. Didn't trust people.'

Together they went next door, into the Control Room, and began the altercation about Toad, Rat, Mole and Badger.

'Before we start...' Skidmore, speaking into a microphone on the computer switch board – the voice coming clear through speakers angled in the four corners of the room. 'Before we start I want everybody to check watches with me. Are you receiving us, Doctor Thirel?'

Klara's voice, disembodied through the

334

speakers, from her eyrie at the defence controls. 'Go ahead. Good luck, Professor.'

'And good luck to you, dear lady. It will be 23.32 at zero. Five. Four. Three. Two. One. Zero.'

Boysie checked the dial on the Breitling Navitimer which came with the diving suit – compliments of Strategic Intelligence. Accurate. Stop watch needles set at zero.

'All ready then, Fortescue?'

The old man jumping up and down, as if on springs, in front of his intricate array of instruments below the screen at the far end of the room. He turned and nodded from the waist, violently. 'Tally-ho. Ban the Bomb. Damn the Mods and Rockers.'

'Up scanner then. Give me some power.'

The solid whine of a generator followed by the shaking of floorboards. Next door the radar scanner was being lifted on to the roof.

Skidmore's hands were moving across the consol as if having a go at the *D minor Toccata and Fugue*. Fortescue, an aged ape at play, nipped smartly among his instruments – patting and caressing. The radar receiver indicators came on – long white arcs of light circling the screens. Then a wide flash over the big wall opposite. Colour. Switzerland,

Italy and the Yugoslavian coast spread before them, mapped in blue, orange, green, black and white. Better focus. Thin dark blue lines moved, crossed and recrossed, patterning the map. In the bottom right corner, sliding up the Adriatic, parallel with the Yugoslavian coastline, a tiny trail of red crept on a steady course heading roughly in the direction of Venice.

'That's the carrier aircraft. The red one – others are commercials. She's there, a little ahead of time, but she's there.' Skidmore like a race commentator. 'What price Fortescue now, Mossfin? All his work, this. All done by mirrors – and the help of photochromic dyes and a few valves, of course. Show us the carrier's turning point then, old lad.'

The map dissolved. In its place a close-up of the Adriatic with details of the two coastlines. The red line advanced towards a prick of light roughly a foot from its apogee.

'That's her turning position – the light about two hundred miles from the Italian coast.'

Boysie was watching Skidmore's head, bending over the console making quick and urgent calculations. 'My god he *is* ahead of time. I shall have to begin running the release tape within seven minutes. We're in a good position now.'

'Go ahead.' Klara on the loudspeaker. 'If she's well positioned go ahead now. We'll cope if they try anything.'

Boysie glanced at his watch. The second hand clocked ten.

'OK.' Skidmore with excitement. 'Right, Fortescue?'

Fortescue glanced toward the console, lips going like a bulldog clip under regular pressure – the sound of words lost in the whine of the generator.

'Give me the release map.'

The screen dissolved and altered again.

'Wonderful things these light-reversible dyes.' The Professor talking to himself.

Genoa was in the top left corner of the screen, the Adriatic bottom right – the carrier aircraft still tracing its neat red stream.

'You ready Mossfin and Boysie?' The big shaggy head turned from the console and grinned – toothy. Boysie raised a limp hand of acknowledgement.

'It only takes a flick of the forefinger.' Skidamore's scrubbed claw hanging over a large central switch. The hand came down and the twin drums of tape began to revolve. 'Tape running. Watch the red line.'

Major Yusykov, at the controls of his TU-20 felt the aircraft buck underneath him. For a moment he thought it was a jet stream. Then the hooded light to the right of his machmeter began to wink. There was a fractional pause before he pushed the plunger – ensuring radio silence and warning his four crewmen that they had slipped into Condition Red. He had long expected this moment. Now it had arrived there was a burst of relief. Tusykoy had come to terms with tension a long time ago. He concentrated, holding the aircraft on course. For a moment he did wonder if there would be reprisals and how soon they would come. His wife and children were on holiday with his parents in the city. Major Tusykov felt his stomach contract. In the nose of the aircraft, signals were coming through the transistorised guidance system and being thrown out again – hurled at *UR/39*.

The red line split on the screen, turning into two definite marks – a V-shaped road junction on a map. The second line moved much faster than its parent.

'She's gone. She's off. We've done stage

one.' Professor Skidmore quite still, hunched over the consol.

The line turned into a fast curve, moving straight and true towards Genoa.

'Give me the final phase map.'

The screen did its dissolving magic again. Zooming close in on Genoa, Voghera, Maggiore, the crimson trail inched its way to Genoa.

One hundred miles south of Genoa the coiled brain of *UR/39* vectored on to its target. The inertial platform tilted. The signal bleeped through at a millionth of a second and the power pack activated the safety device. Fifty miles from the target the vehicle registered its new course. The accelerometers made a minute change and the long silver germ dropped to 20,000 feet and began to lose speed.

'Watch her. Just about now. She should lock about now.'

The line faltered, still creeping forward, slower now. Over Genoa and turning. Turning and thickening – the sign, Skidmore said, that she was reducing height.

'Down to 10,000.'

The line wavered and then seemed to pick

up a scent. Straight towards Voghera beacon and in line with the Isole di Brissago.

'We've got her. By god we've got her. Off you go, Boysie.'

Boysie's reaction was a second behind that of Mostyn. Out of the room, over the scanner lift – metal floor now – across the landing and into the lift. Come on.

'Faster, damn you.' Mostyn brutally to the lift.

Down. Boysie's guts six inches above his head.

'Five. Four. Two. Eight. A stroke CX.' Mostyn beating Boysie again, speaking into the perforated circle. The steel door swooping up. Mostyn away running up the passage. Boysie lumbering behind, not so fast in his rubber suit. Sweat already. Why the hell hadn't they waited down on the hovercraft? Because Skidmore was determined that rotten Mostyn should see Fortescue's brilliant display screen. Up Mostyn. Up Skidmore. Up the both of them with the bloody *Chronic Illness*.

Through the Seniors' wash room – no underwear this time. A twitch of desire. Fear promoting desire. A Senior by the door (long black hair, good thighs and a Sten). Up the stairs. Up. Up. The narrow spiral of stone steps. Church bells. No, that was a century ago. His hand on the safety rope, the big Navitimer round his hairy wrist. 'The man of action uses Schloop's Hair Dressing.' A mustiness in the summer house. Along the path. Cypresses. Mimosa. The water.

Frederick had already started the hover-craft's motors. He jumped clear as Mostyn scrambled down into the cabin. Boysie panting next to him – a shin barked on the metal as he clambered in. 'Swive it.' An oath from Boysie.

The cockpit canopy was pushed right back to give them room for manoeuvre once they got to the missile. Mostyn's hands sure – almost casual – on the controls, phones clamped over his small ears. Boysie cursed Mostyn's easy professionalism, remember-ing his keck-handed attempt with the hovercraft. A switch down. A spear of light from the nose. A push and roar. Vibration as the compressor fans began to whir. Heavy rumble from the airscrew high in the rear. Lift. The light stabbing in front of them as they gathered speed – a long oval skimming across the water. Boysie went through the drill – swivel mounting free on the hand-operated spot they had fitted outside the starboard edge of the cockpit; rope and sling; flippers on, tight round his feet. Uncomfortable. They were ripping out on to the lake, tearing up the water behind them, the island a black splodge to their left.

Mostyn's hand suddenly to his ear. 'Splash-down.' He yelled. 'Splash-down.'

Boysie jumped a couple of inches – keeping level with his heart – and pressed the stop watch plunger on the Navitimer. Mostyn pushing up the revs, one hand down on the compass, setting course from Skidmore's instructions filtering through the earpieces.

At the same moment, two things happened. Behind the island – from the direction of Locarno – a violet flash cut across the sky, followed by a burst of silver stars dropping and arching out, willowing on to the lake surface. The fireworks were beginning. Automatically, Boysie's head turned towards the flash. As it did so his eyes picked up another moving image – on the lake, less than twenty yards away. The noise of motors seemed to have got louder. Boysie's head whipped round again – a double-take on the object – a dark shape moving rapidly away from them, heading into the black mass that was the island, a broad strip of white spreading out behind.

'What the hell's that?' he shouted.

Mostyn lifted an earpiece – irritation round the eyes and forehead. 'Can't hear. What?' Shouting.

Boysie bawled, pointing. 'Over there. What the hell is it?'

Mostyn's head jerked in the direction of Boysie's unsteady finger. Another burst of fireworks – gold, red, green flowers, high, lighting the lake like misty dusk. For five seconds the island was plainly visible – a small open bathing beach on the west side, and, in front, the unmistakable fast shape of a motor boat turning in. Behind the boat, three skiers, straining backwards on their taut ropes. Further out, coming in behind the first lone boat, another formation of three – each with its trailing trio of skiers.

'She's left it too late.' Mostyn yelling on a high note. They banked alarmingly. 'Klara's left it too bloody late.'

As he shouted, the island seemed to explode into a haphazard glare of bright eyes – a battery of searchlights bringing the whole area into dazzling vision. The first boat was completing its turn, coming parallel with the beach and thrusting away, its skiers sliding round in its wake. As they reached the centre of the turn, head-on to the beach, they cast of their ropes – three white skid marks clawing up towards the shore, slowing as the skis lost planing speed, and sinking into the shallow water for a 'dry landing'.

'They're going in on skis.' The obvious bursting out.

'Why the hell doesn't Klara use her barriers. Watch them, Boysie. Must keep on course. You watch them.'

The three other boats were positioning for their turn towards the beach, flying through the water, dead for the shore. Boysie thought he saw the flicker of hand gun fire from the trees near the land spot. Certainly all the lights had now been turned on to this one area. Klara must be operating something. She had said the defences were foolproof. Barriers. Mostyn had shouted. The boats were about fifty yards from the shore, ready to turn, their positioning, in a wide V, immaculate. Boysie craned back, his line of vision splendid between the boats and the island. Without warning, ten yards ahead of the lead boat, a curtain of water rose up – stretching round the whole of the western end of the island in a long curve. The water fell away, leaving what looked like a tall metal grid growing from the lake. A crash barrier. Steel net, eight feet high, sloping outwards. The barricade.

'Bloody hell. Metal things out of the water.'

'That's it.' Mostyn talking like a deaf man on the telephone. 'Steel wire. Dangerous. Set in concrete bunkers, operated hydraulically and electrified. Live for five seconds on contact. Lethal. She's got three of 'em.'

The lead boat was too close to do anything. The man at the wheel probably did not even see the obstruction. They struck the net bows on – wood and metal folding back as if hit by a blow torch. Then a confusion of fire exploding in a tall snake of flame.

The three skiers did not even have a chance to react and drop their lines. In horrific slow unison they were pulled forward – catapulted into mid-air. The centre man kept hanging on – through shock, or perhaps an unconscious clutch at self-preservation. Boysie saw him turn on the rope and disappear into the column of flame. The other two let go – slithering forward out of control, splattering into the barrier in a shower of sparks.

The remaining boats attempted to slow down and turn away – one making it at the expense of his skiers who were dragged suddenly inwards bouncing one after another into the barrier – the line of sparks running and flashing over the whole fence. The other misjudged his turn and hurtled broadside into the metal. Once more the grind, pyramid of fire and flying bodies like somersaulting dolls. Behind, a huge blossom of rockets from Locarno – raining balls of coloured fire against the mountains.

Boysie's stomach felt hollow. The carnage, witnessed in the past few minutes, had about it the ring of unreality. Amid the noise of wind and motors in the cockpit it had been like watching a Technicolor silent film – the effects department responsible for the fire and explosion, stunt men performing their 'derring do' on skis. The bodies, which he knew floated, charred, on the lake, were only dummies. They had to be dummies.

'Crumbs,' he said, an unconscious wish for childhood. 'Bleeding crumbs.' The diving suit felt insufferably hot. Boysie looked down at his watch – only four minutes since Mostyn received the splash-down signal. He glanced back at the island – now receding rapidly (Mostyn batting up the knots). But for one lone spotlight, playing round the area of the beach, the Isole di Brissago were in darkness.

The metal barriers had disappeared and two floating fires marked all that remained of *Assault One's* invasion force.

'Coming up to it.' Mostyn dragged Boysie's mind back to the real issue. 'Switch on that spot, Oaksie. Got your bath salts and plastic ducks?'

Boysie could not think of anything suitably cutting. He swallowed the obvious obscenity and turned on the spot, swinging it forward so that its shaft of light converged with the beam from the fixed lamp in the hovercraft's nose. The *Chronic Illness* was there – about twenty yards ahead. Different from the mock-up which floated so peacefully in the swimming pool, safe among the cellars of the island villa. Boysie did not expect the vehicle to be painted white. He had practised on a silver replica. Somehow, the glowing white bullet, bobbing with one wing low in the water, not the attitude of its facsimile, did not look right. The whiteness and peculiar angle put him off. The watch again. Seven minutes gone. Twenty-three left in which to do the job and get the hell out of the vicinity. Mostyn brought the hovercraft close in on the starboard side, eased back on the throttles and allowed the machine to settle quietly on the water. The missile was only a few feet away and below. Boysie swung the spot on it. He could see the inspection plate as he leaned out over the side of the cockpit.

'Keep the glim on me won't you.' As if to a conspiratorial burglar.

'Don't worry, laddie. For once in your life you'll be in the spotlight. Off you go. Keep in touch.'

Boysie climbed on to the edge of the cockpit, ready for his leap. As it happened, the descent was somewhat ignoble. He launched out, but the dreaded flippers were up to their old tricks – the tip of his right fin catching in the top rung of the fixed ladder which ran down the side of the craft. Boysie's body fell forward and, with an inelegant yelp, he entered the water head first – narrowly missing the missile's swinging wing. Disregarding the sardonic laugh from the cockpit above, Boysie struck out for the white shape.

'It's no more difficult than in the bath. It's no more difficult than in the bloody bath.' He muttered, going through the business of heaving himself up the short wing. It was more difficult, the balance was not the same. The wing seemed filmy with oil. Twice he tried to get into position, slipping each time – the whole missile rolling in a vicious banking movement so that he had to duck to avoid getting a heavy swipe from the wing as it fell and lifted and then fell back into the water again. Third time lucky. As his left arm grasped the top of the fuselage his watch came into vision. Nineteen minutes to go. Screws off the inspection plate. Slower than working on the mock-up. The screws tighter. Six. Seven. The eighth was a bastard. Now the screws on the inner plate. Easy. Mostyn was keeping the light steady. The interior was more complex than he expected. More bits and pieces than in the swimming pool. Twelve terminals in sequence. Trauma. A block in the mind. The beginning of the sequence? Which came first, red terminal or blue? He knew the rest. Damned if he was going to ask Mostyn. Try the red. Russian roulette with terminals. Red? Correct. No bang. All terminals out. Bit of trouble with the black. First canister – the size of a Golden Syrup tin. Out easily. No problems. Fifteen minutes.

'Let's have the rope.' His voice loud in the silence, unbroken except for the splash of water. He grabbed the webbing harness, buckled it round the canister and gave a gentle tug on the rope. The canister lifted away from him. Now the forward tin.

Boysie had just begun to unscrew when he heard a sharp scraping noise. He stopped, a chill sweeping through the sweat under the rubber. The noise again, from the other side of the missile. Then, a faint metallic dragging sound. Pulling himself up, he tried to peer over the fuselage. Ice charged through his carotid arteries, while his scalp seemed to have been dusted with itching powder. As Boysie's eyes came up over the fuselage so another shape rose from the far side of the missile. A head, rubber-hooded, like his own, but the face obscured by a *Nemrod* mask.

Apart from the natural symptoms of shock, Boysie's first instinct was one of intense fury. Someone else was trying to get into *his* missile from the other side.

'What the bloody...?'

'I shouldn't bother, Mr Oakes. Just giving you a hand. We felt it might be important to salvage the canisters. We don't want the wrong people to get them.' He knew the voice. Somewhere recently. The thing from the lake spoke again. 'If you're thinking of being silly I should take a look at your friend.'

Boysie twisted his head, moving to get out of the glare from the spot. Mostyn leaned over the side of the hovercraft cockpit. He hunched his shoulders, lifting his palms upwards in a 'that's life' gesture, Behind him stood a large young man wearing a polo-neck sweater. The young man had an Avtomat Kalashnikov rifle stuck in Mostyn's ear. Above them, sitting like Humpty Dumpty on the cockpit canopy, was Kadjawaji.

'I've been looking forward to this, Boysie Oakes. Since the train.'

Boysie was tempted to the 'Har-har so we meet again' bit.

'Get on, Boysie Oakes. I don't mind you being here for the bang.' The thin, hideous voice ended in a cackle. 'But we'd rather like to leave before then.'

It was all too much. Boysie looked from the frogman to Kadjawaji, to Mostyn and back to Kadjawaji.

'Still got your air pistol?' Was all his brain could signal to the vocal chords.

'It's right here and I can use it if you like. Our friend will finish the work. I apologise for being so old fashioned – using an air pistol of such power.' There was a 'pfutt' from Kadjawaji's right hand (the sling had disappeared) and something clanged into the wing an inch or to from Boysie's leg. Kadjawaji cackled again – the squeal of an animal in pain. 'Old but effective. They make the darts specially for me. Nice engineering with a unique draining device for the curare. Get on with it, Oakes.' The miniman drummed his legs on the side of the cockpit.

'I should do as he says.' The voice from the other side of the fuselage. Boysie turned. The merman lifted his mask. It was St Peter – the concierge from the *Palmira*.

Boysie wanted to scream. It was so unfair. He had never asked for this. You just could not trust anybody in this game.

'Please, Mr Oakes.' St Peter could have been speaking to him from behind the reception desk. 'I will deal with the canister on this side. We haven't much time left I'm sure.'

There was nothing Boysie could do. He had to play for time. They never gave him time to think. A few weeks in the Bahamas with sand trickling through his toes; palm trees and time to do nothing but think. His mind did its usual grasshopper stunt – leaping from stupid idea to stupid idea. The process ended nowhere. Half-heartedly Boysie settled down to unscrewing the second canister.

'I bet you had a good laugh at me then.' Dismally, he called to St Peter.

'On the contrary. Truly I'm sorry about this. I did everything I could to stop it. Sent a message back to my control. Obviously he did not get it in time. They would have stopped the flight or something. The trouble is we are never kept fully in the picture. If I'd only known who Miss Wheater really was...'

Boysie had the canister out and was strapping it into the webbing. He pulled on the rope and Mostyn heave-hoed it into the cockpit.

'I have the other one.' St Peter leaned over the missile, the last canister in his outstretched hand. Boysie noticed there were six minutes to go. He took the canister.

'I'm sorry about your Member of Parliament,' said St Peter quietly. 'That was on orders from my control. Penton was getting nervous and difficult. There was going to be trouble. I'm sure you would have done the same if ordered.'

'You did him?'

'I helped him. Yes.'

'Over his balcony you helped him?'

'Unhappily, yes.'

'Well for god's sake don't tell my boss. He thinks I did it.' He had the canister now. The webbing dangled from the cockpit. Boysie felt utterly defeated. He had rather taken to

St Peter.

'Brothers under our skin,' he muttered foolishly, and buckled the canister into place. This time his eyes followed it on its journey upwards. Mostyn leaned forward, lifted the canister, then, in one movement, swung round. Kadjawaji screamed as the tin hit his arm (it must have still been painful) – the air pistol, clattering down the side of the hovercraft. Mostyn followed through, still turning, bringing the guard's AK rifle muzzle over his right shoulder, nudging it away with his chin as he began to spit. His right arm continued to sweep upwards and the rifle stopped firing – the guard falling backwards, jaw cracking under the perfect right hook. All this in one flowing movement. At the same time, Mostyn was yelling, 'Come on. Come on, Boysie.' His left hand under the unconscious guard's knees, tipping him out of the cockpit.

Boysie slid off the wing. The whole of the *Chronic Illness* pitched with him, almost turning turtle. St Peter gave a surprised cry (like a sealion's bark, Boysie thought afterwards) as he lost hold and slipped back into the lake. Boysie saw his wing swing up again, and heard its partner on the far side, hit something, on its downward sweep, with

354

a harsh crack. He did not wait to find out what it was – flailing out, making for the hovercraft. Hands on the bottom rung of the ladder, then pulling up, shaking and prising the fins from his feet. Over the side of the cockpit now. Mostyn back at the controls. Motors from idling to power. Above them Kadjawaji still clung to the canopy.

'Pistol on the floor, Boysie.'

Boysie already had Mostyn's automatic in his hand, thumb flicking it from safe to fire, turning to deal with Kadjawaji – there was no sentiment, no fear and no worry about killing the dwarf. But Kadjawaji had not spent four years in a circus for nothing. The little man was standing, balanced on top of the cockpit – running back along the spine of the hovercraft. Boysie pulled himself up as the dwarf turned to face him.

'Go on,' screamed the dwarf through the motor's roar, inviting the bullet. Boysie lifted the pistol – the notch of the backsight in line with the foresight blade, both held steady on the little black face. It was no good. A sitting duck. He could not. Not at a sitting duck. Boysie tried again and thought he read terror in the button white eyes as Kadjawaji backed away. Mostyn was turning the craft, setting course for the islands.

Kadjawaji had retreated as far as the airscrew pedestal, hanging on with one baby hand. Boysie filled his lungs and hauled himself on to the top of the canopy. As his knees made contact with the smooth plexiglass surface he saw Kadjawaji move again.

'Stop. For Chrissake...' The warning died at the same moment as the dwarf. Instinct to withdraw from danger was so great that his mind had not taken in the large peril of the spinning airscrew. The blade tips just reached down to Kadjawaji's head. The dwarf spun off the side of the craft in a disgusting flurry of blood and tissue. Boysie retched. There was nothing else.

He slid back into the cockpit. Two of the canisters lay in the well of his bucket seat – the other rolled around the floor. Tenderly, he placed the three tins together in front of the seat into which he dropped. Turning, he looked back, Somewhere in the blackness a small mushroom of flame was dying on the lake's surface. The stop watch showed exactly thirty minutes since it had been set.

Some four minutes later he spoke. 'Thank you.'

'Not at all.' Mostyn, frozen and keeping distance between master and slave as only

the British upper crust can. 'Thank *you.*
Combined effort. Sorry they jumped me.
Must have followed us out. Didn't hear a
thing until that goon stuck a rifle in...'

'Your earhole.'

'My ear.'

As they rounded the western end of the
island Mostyn said. 'You know what I fancy,
old Oakes? You know what I really fancy?'

'No. What do you fancy?' An old time
music hall act.

'A slice of that Klara Thirel.' Wicked leer.

'You would. You bloody would. You'd
make a peach of a pair.'

EMERALD EPILOGUE: BRISSAGO. LOCARNO. LONDON

Being congratulated by Skidmore – Boysie considered – was like engaging in playful combat with a bear. The old man hugged, slapped backs and pumped hands with aggressive vigour, while Fortescue danced round the canisters muttering, 'That'll learn 'em. Damned Mods and Rockers.'

Klara was talking intimate Italian to some police inspector in Locarno. One of her girls, she said, thought two motor boats had collided at speed off the island. Everyone looked pleased, and Boysie decided that it was better not to enquire into the fate of the three skiers who had actually got on to the beach. As like as not Klara would have them chained up – pets in the cellarage.

A Senior escorted him to *Il Portone* – to the room prepared for him. He washed, depressed and uneasy, then made his way back, down the lift shaft for the last time, up the tunnel, across the gymnasium to Klara's study. High jinks were in progress, with the whisky flowing. Boysie had a couple of doubles and then made his excuses.

'See you in the morning, old Boysie,' said Mostyn not taking his eyes off Klara.

'Goodnight, Boysie,' said Klara, not taking her eyes off Mostyn.

Fortescue, collapsed in a chair waved a skinny hand. 'Rods and Mockers.'

They left *Il Portone* at ten the next day – driven by Angela in Klara's Victor.

'How did you get on with Klara?'

'Shut up,' said Mostyn, sharply.

Mostyn waited in the car outside the *Palmira* while Boysie went in to collect his luggage and pay the bill. He walked across the gilded foyer, head down, not looking at anybody. Suddenly he had an aversion to locking eyes with people.

'Good mornink, Mr Oakes.'

Boysie's head jerked up. St Peter stood smiling behind the reception desk, a large piece of sticking plaster decorating his brow.

'I didn't ... I ... bu-bu-butohh-bu?'

'No, sir. I was supposed to have the week-end off. But they are short-staffed. What can you do? I had hoped to go Scuba diving.'

'I didn't know there were any Scuba in the lake.' Boysie, dead, and buried, pan. 'Are you all right?'

'A slight headache.' Then, quietly, 'Congratulations.'

'Someone has to win.'

'True.' St Peter's lips parted in a great big dentifrice grin. 'And, after all, it is only half-time. Wait until the game is over.'

Boysie decided that he would not mention St Peter to Mostyn. That was his own secret. His bit of private information. Besides, they were on neutral ground.

As Angela drove them towards the railway station, Boysie caught a glimpse of Griffin, sitting perkily at one of the tables outside the *Muralo* – deep in chat with a middle-aged blonde.

'Funny,' said Mostyn.

'What?'

'Nothing really. Just thought I saw old Charlie Griffin outside that hotel back there.'

'Griffin?'

'You wouldn't remember him. I pointed him out to you – years ago. Funny though. Had an idea he was ill. 'Flu or something.'

Boysie thought his bowels were going to strangle his lungs.

He got back to the flat off Chesham Place – weak and shaky after the flight from

Zürich – at eight minutes past nine. On the mat lay three bills and a postcard. The postcard bore Elizabeth's round scrawl.

I'm not. Hooray. Please, please call me as soon as you get back. Sandy's found a super Italian restaurant in Chancery Lane. Love. E.

Boysie rang. Elizabeth would be round in half an hour. He put the kettle on and began to run a bath. The doorbell pinged just as he was taking off his shirt. Petronella stood in the hall – beauty-cared, coiffured, and clad in an expensive emerald model.

'Ah,' said Boysie.

'Hallo, darling. I came on the off-chance that you were back.' A pout. 'Hoped we could finish what we started yesterday.'

'Ah,' said Boysie again. This, he thought, had nothing on Kadjawaji or Amber Nine, or even Hector. Two birds converging. Collision courses.

'Hurry up, Boysie,' called Petronella from the bedroom.

PURPLE POSTSCRIPT: LONDON

'You're a sloth, Boysie lad. A sloth.'

Mostyn had come in quietly, knocking Boysie's feet off the desk, causing him to jump and drop the copy of *The Times* which he was quickly reconnoitring during Mostyn's absence.

It had been a hard, nervy six weeks since their return from Switzerland. Rumour, tension, threats of Royal Commissions and the continual coming and going of smooth young men in overcoats with velvet collars.

'Good morning, sir.'

'It's a horrible morning and what the hell's this?' Mostyn picking up a large card from the top of his mail, stacked tidily on the desk. 'Lord, has that come round again?'

'What, sir?'

'Department's Fancy Dress Dinner.'

'Oh yes. That. I've had one. Going, sir?'

'I shall go,' said Mostyn with precision, 'as a fancy dress ball. A purple fancy dress ball.' He dropped the card back on to his desk. 'And what do you find so interesting in *The*

Times newspaper, my Boysie boy?'

'Just looking through the Court Circular, and Births and Deaths, sir. Oh I did notice that Professor Skidmore's been appointed to a Chair at one of the Californian universities. He left the organisation?'

'Hadn't you heard?'

'What?'

'Strategic Intelligence has been disbanded.'

'What? After Amber Nine? After that?'

'Especially after that. You know what was in those bloody canisters?'

'Germs?'

'Deadly. NaC1. CaCo3 and a preparation of Bi.'

'That bad? I mean. Grief. What are they?'

'In plain language. Salt, chalk and bismuth.'

'You mean...?'

Mostyn nodded. 'Ingrid's word got through. They played little jokies on us. And their own people, come to that. They just don't care.'

'But...' Boysie thought of the slaughter.

'It's all in the game, Boysie. Something for nothing. Life for laughs. Death for a handful of salt, a piece of chalk and a powder to soothe your guts.'

The publishers hope that this book has given you enjoyable reading. Large Print Books are especially designed to be as easy to see and hold as possible. If you wish a complete list of our books please ask at your local library or write directly to:

Magna Large Print Books
Magna House, Long Preston,
Skipton, North Yorkshire.
BD23 4ND